Series A
Advent•Christmas•Epiphany

Study Guide

By Richard Wolkenhauer
and Lester Seto
Edited by Thomas J. Doyle

Assistant to the editor: Cindi Anderson

Write to the Library for the Blind, 1333 S. Kirkwood Road, St. Louis, MO 63122-7295 to obtain this study in braille or large print for the visually impaired.

Scripture quotations are taken from THE HOLY BIBLE: NEW INTERNATIONAL VERSION®. Copyright © 1973, 1978, 1984 by the International Bible Society. Used by permission of Zondervan Publishing House. All rights reserved.

The "NIV" and "New International Version" are registered in the United States Patent and Trademark Office by the International Bible Society. Use of either trademark requires the permission of the International Bible Society.

Scripture quotations marked KJV are from the King James or Authorized Version of the Bible.

Reference marked *LW* are from *Lutheran Worship,* copright © 1982. By permission of Concordia Publishing House.

Copyright © 1995 Concordia Publishing House
3558 South Jefferson Avenue, St. Louis, MO 63118-3968
Manufactured in the United States of America

All rights reserved. No part of this publication may be reproduced, stored in a retrieval system, or transmitted, in any form or by any means, electronic, mechanical, photocopying, recording or otherwise, without the prior written permission of Concordia Publishing House.

Contents

Introduction	4
Session 1: First Sunday in Advent Get Ready for Jesus!	5
Session 2: Second Sunday in Advent Roots in Paradise!	12
Session 3: Third Sunday in Advent Are We There Yet?	18
Session 4: Fourth Sunday in Advent Who's in Charge?	25
Session 5: The Nativity of Our Lord Appearances Count—They Really Do!	31
Session 6: First Sunday after Christmas Always in Jeopardy … But Never in Jeopardy	38
Session 7: Second Sunday after Christmas Saying "Amen" to God	45
Session 8: The Epiphany of Our Lord What's the Big Attraction?	51
Session 9: The Baptism of Our Lord Water and the Word	58
Session 10: Second Sunday after the Epiphany Called Instead of Condemned	64
Session 11: Third Sunday after the Epiphany The Gloom of Darkness, the Joy of Light	71
Session 12: Fourth Sunday after the Epiphany God Creates a Humble Heart	76
Session 13: Fifth Sunday after the Epiphany Living the Faith	82
Session 14: Sixth Sunday after the Epiphany The Letter of the Law, the Spirit of the Law	89
Session 15: Seventh Sunday after the Epiphany The Perfect Son of God	95
Session 16: Eighth Sunday after the Epiphany Who Cares? God Does!	100
Session 17: The Transfiguration of Our Lord Christ's Majesty and Mercy	108

Introduction

About the Series

This course is 1 of 12 in the Church Year series. The Bible studies in this series are tied to the 3-year lectionary. These studies allow participants to explore the Old Testament lesson (or lesson from the book of Acts during the Easter season), the Epistle lesson, and the Gospel lesson appointed for each Sunday of the church year. Also, optional studies give participants the opportunity to study in-depth the lessons appointed for festival days during the church year that fall on days other than Sunday (e.g., Christmas Eve, Christmas Day, Epiphany, Maundy Thursday, Good Friday, Ascension, Reformation).

Book 1 for years A, B, and C in the lectionary series will include 17 studies for the Scripture lessons appointed for the Sundays and festival days in Advent, Christmas, and Epiphany. Book 2 will include 17 studies for the lessons appointed for the Sundays and festival days in Lent and Easter and for the lessons appointed for Ascension and Pentecost. Book 3 (15 sessions) and 4 (16 sessions) will include studies that focus on the lessons appointed for the Pentecost season.

After a brief review and textual study of the Scripture lessons appointed for a Sunday or festival day, each study is designed to help participants draw conclusions about each of the lessons, compare the lessons, discover a unifying theme in the lessons (if possible), and apply the theme to their lives. At the end of each study, the Scripture lessons for the next Sunday and/or festival day are assigned in preparation for the next study. The leaders guide for each course provides additional information on appointed lessons, answers to the questions in the study guide, a suggested process for teaching the study, and devotional or worship activities tied to the theme.

May the Holy Spirit richly bless you as you study God's Word!

Session 1

First Sunday in Advent

Isaiah 2:1–5; Romans 13:11–14; Matthew 24:37–44

Focus

Theme: *Get Ready For Jesus!*

Law/Gospel Focus

The failure to keep God's Law can bring fear, anxiety, and guilt as we anticipate God's final judgment. God assures us in His Word that through faith in Jesus He has prepared us to meet Jesus when He returns as judge. We have nothing to fear. Instead, we look forward to Christ's return as a day of deliverance and salvation.

Objectives

By the power of the Holy Spirit working through God's Word we will
1. examine the tension between the biblical warnings concerning the end and Christ's promises of deliverance on the Last Day;
2. rejoice in the blessings of this life and the next as people who have been clothed in the righteousness of Jesus Christ;
3. avoid the Santa Claus mentality of evaluating human worth based upon people's goodness.

Opening Worship

Four violet or blue votive candles serve as the visual focus for the worship during these four Advent weeks. At the lighting of the initial candle—the Prophecy candle—recite together the common table prayer:

> Come, Lord Jesus, be our Guest,
> And let Thy gifts to us be blest. Amen!

Meditate silently upon this "Advent Prayer" to weigh the abundance of God's gifts to us. Sing or speak together stanzas 1–4 of "The Advent of Our God" (*LW* 12).

> The advent of our God
> Shall be our theme for prayer;
> Come, let us meet Him on the road
> And place for Him prepare.
>
> The everlasting Son
> Incarnate stoops to be,
> Himself the servant's form puts on
> To set His people free.
>
> Come, Zion's daughter, rise
> To meet your lowly King,
> Nor let your faithless heart despise
> The peace He comes to bring.
>
> As judge, on clouds of light,
> He soon will come again
> And all His scattered saints unite
> With Him on high to reign.

Introduction

Already the mad rush to prepare for the celebration of Christmas is underway. We are warned to shop early and to count down the shopping days until Christmas.

1. What other evidence can you provide that you or others are in a mad rush to get ready for Christmas?

Setting materialism aside, there remains another, more insidious idea imbedded in our preparation for Christmas—the notion that human goodness readies people for blessings and reward. Children are warned to be good and to watch out " ... for Santa Claus is coming to town ... He's making a list and checking it twice, gonna find out who's naughty or nice ... Santa Claus is coming to town."

2. What danger lurks in promoting the message in this favorite song?

Though there is much preparation to be made, it is *God who prepares the way* for us in His love. The very sights and sounds of our preparation for Christmas can distract us from the divine Advent call that beckons us to celebrate not merely a holiday but to get ready for that Holy Day when Christ will return again to earth, not as a baby, but as the King.

3. Compare the *true* preparation for celebrating Jesus' first coming to earth and Christ's return to this earth a second time with the preparation promoted when we sing, "Santa Claus is coming to town."

God alone prepares us through faith to worship our Savior born in Bethlehem. God alone prepares us to meet Christ the King who will return to judge the living and the dead.

4. Considering these facts, what might you do this year to celebrate Jesus' first coming? His second coming?

===================== **Inform** =====================

Isaiah 2:1–5—Isaiah holds before us the hope of an "end time" that will usher in an end to hatred and war. Peace will reign. To those who follow the "ways" God teaches, His grace and mercy will put an end to all troubles.

Romans 13:11–14—Paul, through inspiration by the Holy Spirit, also treats "Judgment Day" as a time of salvation for us as God's redeemed people. He calls us to a life of faith that casts aside the immorality of this world and puts on the armor of light that enables us to behave decently as those who through faith have clothed ourselves with the Lord Jesus Christ.

Matthew 24:37–44—At first glance, this text may seem frightening. The world rushes toward doom! But there is hope: through faith God rescued Noah and His family. In a similar way God will rescue us who are "ready" through faith in Jesus from His judgment toward sin—death. By grace through faith we stand before Christ when He returns as those He has redeemed—those for whom He has earned the crown of life.

1. Skim the Scripture lessons appointed for this day. Then skim the first chapters of the gospels according to Matthew, Mark, and Luke. Identify differences and similarities between Jesus first coming in Bethlehem to His second coming. Write the similarities and differences on the chart.

Jesus' First Coming and Jesus' Second Coming

Similarities	Differences

2. Which coming do you most eagerly celebrate—the first or the second? Why?

3. Compare the words of Isaiah 2:3–5 with the message of the angels who appeared to the shepherds, "Glory to God in the highest, and on earth peace to men on whom His favor rests" (Luke 2:14).

4. Jesus first came to give us peace. This peace we have *now* through faith. Jesus will come again to give us peace. This peace we

have *not yet,* but will receive someday through faith. How can we have peace from Jesus *now* and *not yet?*

5. Paul reminds us to "put on the armor of light" and "clothe yourselves with the Lord Jesus Christ." It may seem from this admonition that we can *do something on our own* to prepare for Jesus' second coming. We must follow principles for interpreting Scripture—read the passage in context and Scripture interprets Scripture—in order to understand fully God's message. Read and then summarize the following passages to better understand Paul's command to "put on" and "clothe."
Romans 3:22–26

Romans 5:1–5

Romans 5:6–11

Romans 6:3–14

Romans 7:21–25

Romans 8:26–27

Romans 8:38–39

6. Quiz yourself now on your preparedness to meet Jesus when He returns again. Tell whether each statement is true or false.
_____ I can look forward to Jesus' second coming because He has prepared me through faith to meet Him.
_____ I have put on the armor of light through faith.

    _____ God clothed me with Christ Jesus through faith.
    _____ Through faith God has prepared me to meet Jesus on Judgment Day.
    _____ Through faith I have nothing to fear when Jesus returns again.

7. If it is through faith in Jesus that God has prepared you for Judgment Day, how can you "Keep watch"? Why would you need to "Keep watch"?

8. Why does the message of the Old Testament lesson, the Epistle lesson, and the Gospel lesson have such an urgency?

Connect

1. Why are so many people preoccupied with trying to date the time of our Lord's return? Would you really want to know exactly when Jesus is going to return in glory? For what good reason might Jesus want to keep this secret?

2. Do you think our day and age is actually more evil than the world of the apostle Paul? Here is Paul's list (Romans 13:13). What might you want to add or subtract from it given our perspective of life today?
    orgies
    drunkenness
    sexual immorality
    debauchery
    dissension
    jealousy

3. What in your celebration of this season addresses Christian life and hope? Justice and judgment? What things distract you from the divine message?

4. How can our congregation foster Christian readiness and hope in this day and age?

5. How might our preparation to once again greet Jesus—the child born in Bethlehem—enable us to prepare ourselves and others to greet Jesus when He returns again?

Vision

During This Week

Evaluate your preparation for Christmas. Identify some ways in which God might better prepare you to celebrate the birth of His Son and to get ready for His return.

Closing Worship

Pray or sing together "Oh, Come, Oh, Come, Emmanuel (*LW* 1).
> Oh, come, oh, come, Emmanuel,
> And ransom captive Israel,
> That mourns in lowly exile here
> Until the Son of God appear.
> Rejoice! Rejoice! Emmanuel
> Shall come to you, O Israel.

Scripture Lessons for Next Sunday

Read in preparation for the Second Sunday in Advent Isaiah 11:1–10; Romans 15:4–13; and Matthew 3:1–12.

Session 2

Second Sunday in Advent

Isaiah 11:1–10; Romans 15:4–13; Matthew 3:1–12

Focus

Theme: *Roots in Paradise!*

Law/Gospel Focus

John the Baptizer has a stern warning from God for those who do not repent. The axe is already laid to the root of the trees, and every tree that does not produce good fruit will be cut down and thrown into the fire. God's judgment awaits all who continue to live secure in their sin and are unwilling to repent and receive the gift of saving faith. Through His Spirit, God calls all to repent and to receive His gift of faith in Christ Jesus. Rooted in faith, the God of hope will fill you with joy and peace, so that you may overflow with hope.

Objectives

By the power of the Holy Spirit working through God's Word we will
1. confess that we who are rooted in Christ, the "root of Jesse" (KJV), God empowers to lead fruitful, productive lives in service to Him;
2. realize that people who are rooted in sin lead lives that are doomed to eternal death;
3. describe the life of one who is rooted in Christ Jesus;
4. affirm the Advent message that the final coming of Christ will affirm both the judgment and the grace of God.

Opening Worship

Speak responsively the Introit for this Sunday.

Leader: Restore us, O God;
Participants: Make Your face shine upon us, that we may be saved.
Leader: Hear us, O Shepherd of Israel, You who lead Joseph like a flock;
Participants: You who sit enthroned between the cherubim.
Leader: You brought a vine out of Egypt;
Participants: And it took root and filled the land.
Leader: Restore us, O God Almighty;
Participants: Make Your face shine upon us, that we may be saved.
Leader: Glory be to the Father and to the Son and to the Holy Spirit;
Participants: As it was in the beginning, is now, and will be forever. Amen
Leader: Restore us, O God;
Participants: Make Your face shine upon us, that we may be saved.

Sing or speak together "Come, O Long-Expected Jesus" (*LW 22*).

> Come, O long expected Jesus,
> Born to set Your people free;
> From our fears and sins release us
> By Your death on Calvary.
> Israel's strength and consolation,
> Hope to all the earth impart,
> Dear desire of ev'ry nation,
> Joy of ev'ry longing heart.
>
> Born Your people to deliver,
> Born a child and yet a king;
> Born to reign in us forever,
> Now Your gracious kingdom bring.
> By Your own eternal Spirit
> Rule in all our hearts alone;
> By Your all sufficient merit
> Raise us to Your glorious throne.

Introduction

Many people spend time seeking their roots. They longingly look back on their ethnic past. They devise family trees. They sense that these roots shape who and what they are.

Our roots are not merely human. We can trace them back to God through the divine creation of Adam and Eve. More important, through faith, we as Christians are rooted in Christ! As Israel in Psalm 80 (the Introit of our opening worship) saw its roots in the redemptive act of God freeing them from their bondage in Egypt, so we have our roots in the redemption earned for us through Christ Jesus. These roots have shaped us and nurtured us in the life and faith of the church as much as our human roots have affected our very being.

The lessons for this Sunday deal with our roots, good and bad, and with Jesus, "the root of Jesse" (KJV).

1. What in your roots has shaped you physically?

2. What personality traits do you recognize as being like that of your ancestors?

3. In your opinion what shapes us most, heredity or environment?

4. Think of an unbecoming or undesireable personal attribute you possess. Can you do anything to change this attribute?

5. What attributes do you possess because of your rootedness in Christ?

Inform

As you read the three lessons, highlight or underline the word *root* or *roots*. Where is the word used in a good sense? In an evil sense? Dig into our passages for a few minutes.

Isaiah 11:1–10—Isaiah longingly looks to the day in which Jesse, David's father, would have a "righteous branch," the Messiah, sprout from his lineage and be empowered by the Holy Spirit to usher in a new age of rightness and righteousness. Even children and wild beasts will romp safely together. In this glorious "new heaven and earth," we, the redeemed, shall live forever with God.

Romans 15:4–13—Here Paul calls upon us who are bound for eternity to live our lives accepting one another, just as Christ accepts us. Our rootedness in Christ provides us unity.

Matthew 3:1–12—John the Baptizer proclaims a new-mindedness in view of the impending "kingdom of heaven." People responded by being baptized and confessing their sins. Out of this redemptive act were to come the fruits (behavior) appropriate to the believers in the Messiah. The roots of human existence were no longer simply ethnic (Abrahamic, in this instance), but Messianic. Where humans produce evil fruit, the impending axe of judgment swings.

1. Does this biblical concept of "roots" rule out human responsibility? Are we driven solely by our roots?

2. Can you find the six or more references to the Spirit in these lessons? What does the Spirit have to do with our bearing good fruit, our rootedness?

3. Although human roots (ethnicity) may divide us, our divine roots (in Christ) unite us. Explain this on the basis of our texts.

4. Is the Advent ("coming") of our Lord cause for elation or for fear? Why?

5. How might we encourage people to be more reflective of their "heavenly roots" than their "family trees"?

Connect

1. How might this Advent season become a time of preparation for you and your loved ones?

2. How might you explain your rootedness in Christ to a fellow believer? an unbeliver?

3. How might you demonstrate your rootedness in Christ by your words and actions?

4. The roots of plants absorb nutrients so that the plant can become strong and produce fruit. What nutrients are necessary for your faith to grow and to remain strong so that you might bear fruit? See 2 Timothy 3:14–17 and 1 Corinthians 11:26.

5. Share with a partner your picture of heaven. How will heaven be different than earth? Review the lessons for today to capture a glimpse of heaven.

6. How shall Christians with roots in heaven live here in the present? Try to find your answers in the texts. What Advent doings of your congregation foster and give opportunity for such a life?

Vision

During This Week
Make a Christian family tree. Who was the "spiritual father or mother" who brought you to the faith? What "spiritual offspring" do you have who came to the faith in part through your own witness and life?

Closing Worship
The second Advent candle is typically the "Bethlehem Candle," symbolic of human preparation to receive and cradle the incarnate Christ. Relight this candle and ponder how the Christ is received and cradled by God's people today. Close with a prayer of thanks for the Christ Child.

Scripture Lessons for Next Sunday
Read in preparation for the Third Sunday in Advent Isaiah 35:1–10; James 5:7–10; and Matthew 11:2–11.

Session 3

Third Sunday in Advent

Isaiah 35:1–10; James 5:7–10; Matthew 11:2–11

Focus

Theme: *Are We There Yet?*

Law/Gospel Focus

Sin causes us to doubt God and to grow impatient with His timetable. God assures us in His Word that just as He kept the promises of the Old Testament prophets in the sending of a Messiah, Jesus Christ, so He keeps every promise He makes. Through faith in the promised Messiah we are not only forgiven for our doubt and impatience, but we are also enabled to be more patient and trusting of God in persecution and trouble.

Objectives

That by the power of the Holy Spirit working through God's Word we will
1. confess that as Christians we sometimes grow impatient with God;
2. rejoice that God kept His promise of sending a Messiah, Jesus Christ, to redeem all people;
3. give thanks that God empowers us by His love and forgiveness to be more patient;
4. rejoice in the knowledge that Jesus will return again to judge the living and the dead.

Opening Worship

Once again use the Advent wreath. This week light three of the candles. The third candle is traditionally known as the "Shepherds' Candle." It reminds us of Jesus, the Good Shepherd, who laid down His life for the sheep.

Take a few moments to practice speaking together the verse from this Sunday's Introit, "Righteousness goes before Him and prepares the way for His steps," in preparation for the responsive reading. These words summarize Jesus' overriding concern for His journey to the cross.

Leader: In Bethlehem, shepherds witnessed the coming of Christ into a world of selfishness and brokenness:
Participants: Righteousness goes before Him and prepares the way for His steps.
Leader: The unjust suffering that was to be heaped upon this incarnate Son of God would have driven a mere mortal to bitterness and lashing out.
Participants: Righteousness goes before Him and prepares the way for His steps.
Leader: Still the Son of God and Son of Man did not journey through life complaining about His fate.
Participants: Righteousness goes before Him and prepares the way for His steps.
Leader: He came to heal the sick, encourage the weak, gladden the brokenhearted, forgive the very enemies of God.
Participants: Righteousness goes before Him and prepares the way for His steps.
Leader: He bids us, as the sons and daughters of His Father, to walk with Him in such a life.
Pariticpants: Righteousness goes before Him and prepares the way for His steps.

Sing or speak together "Savior, Thy Dying Love" (*LW* 374).

> Savior, Thy dying love
> Thou gavest me;
> Nor should I aught withhold,
> Dear, Lord, from Thee.
> In love my soul would bow,
> My heart fulfill its vow,
> Some off'ring bring Thee now,
> Something for Thee.
>
> O'er the blest mercy seat,
> Pleading for me,

My feeble faith looks up,
Jesus, to Thee.
Help me the cross to bear,
Thy wondrous love declare,
Some song to raise or prayer,
Something for Thee.

Give me a faithful heart,
Likeness to Thee,
That each departing day
Henceforth may see
Some work of love begun,
Some deed of kindness done,
Some wand'rer sought and won,
Something for Thee.

All that I am and have,
Thy gifts so free,
In joy, in grief, through life,
Dear Lord, for Thee!
And when Thy face I see,
My ransomed soul shall be
Through all eternity
Something for Thee.

Introduction

Patience, it appears, is hard to come by these days! The crowded scenes of modern life test our endurance. Long lines stymie us at the store; traffic slows our journey; reservations not withstanding, we are made to tarry at the restaurant. Children can often give us the most apropos example of impatience; on a lengthy trip the plaintive cry, "Are we there yet?" is heard repeatedly. Similarly, as "children of the Kingdom" we can become so obsessed with the arrival that we do not handle life's journey very well.

1. Share a recent time when you grew impatient as you waited.

2. What factors in life drive us to become impatient?

3. How might you describe life with Christ in terms of a journey?

4. How does Christ's life of patient endurance and His slow and agonizing death on the cross help us on our journey to heaven when we ask in frustration "Are we there yet?"

Inform

Scan the brief summaries of the Scripture lessons for the Third Sunday in Advent. As you study the lessons note the importance of patience.

Isaiah 35:1–10—Isaiah prophesies of a day when those held in Babylonian captivity would be freed by the Persians under King Cyrus (538 B.C.). Such redemption will cause the people of God to sing and rejoice as they march in Jerusalem (35:10). But this will just be the beginning of the fulfillment of Isaiah 35. Something ever greater will happen! The promised Messiah, Jesus Christ, will heal the blind and the lame, the deaf and the mute, and feeble hands will be strengthened and weak knees steadied (Isaiah 35:3, 5–6; Matthew 11:5). These things would be evidence that Jesus was the promised Savior of all people; He was the one who would atone for their sin with His own life, death, and resurrection. However, the fulfillment of Isaiah's prophesy would demand patience.

James 5:7–10—James reminds his readers that though they are being persecuted they can look forward to the Lord's second coming and His judgment. He illustrates the need for patience by reminding them of a farmer who is patient as he waits on God to bring about a harvest once the seed has been planted. Immediately following the text, Job is cited as an example of someone who patiently trusted God in the midst of trouble and turmoil.

Matthew 11:2–11—John the Baptizer has been unjustly imprisoned by Herod Antipas. In his imprisonment John wonders if he is waiting for the right things, and so he instructs his disciples to ask Jesus an important question: "Are You the one who was to come, or should we expect someone else?" Jesus' answer was simply that they were to report what they had seen and heard. The prophets had predicted that the promised Messiah would do exactly what He had been doing—miracles and healing, including the raising of the dead and the preaching of the Good News to the poor.

God promises to act to restore His people. However, patience is required. God's timetable is often very different than ours.

1. Compare the horrors of Isaiah 34:5–17 with the rejoicing of Isaiah 35.

2. Describe the scene of the people of God once they were redeemed from exile (35:9–10). Why do you think Isaiah 35:10 is repeated in Isaiah 51:11?

3. Isaiah speaks also of the redemption which is to take place with the coming of the Messiah, Jesus Christ. When will final restoration be given to God's people (Romans 8:22–23)?

4. Why should the promise of the Lord's second coming bring comfort to the readers of James' epistle? See James 5:1–6.

5. What is the relationship between faith and patience?

6. What evidence is there that John is becoming more and more impatient (Matthew 11:2–3)? Why did John's imprisonment multiply his impatience?

7. What evidence did Jesus give that He was the promised Messiah (Matthew 11:4–6)? See also Isaiah 29:18–21; 35:5–6; 61:1.

================ **Connect** ================

1. Do you consider yourself a patient person? How do you think others view you? Are you an "Are we there yet?" type?

2. Can you think of some "prisons" in your life that have made you very impatient with God? Like John the Baptizer, did you or do you have doubts regarding God's timetable? During these times, where have you found encouragement?

3. Are you simply born with patience as a virtue? Because we're not by nature patient, what did God do? See Galatians 4:4–5. How does one acquire the gift of patience? See Galatians 5:22.

4. Is doctor-assisted suicide a sign of the impatience of our times? Describe some other telltale signs that people are becoming more and more impatient.

5. How can this holy season of Advent help to foster patience for the child of God?

6. Explain how the very situation that makes people impatient can become an arena for ministry of patient endurance.

Vision

During This Week

There was a time when many of the highways of Indiana were marked with crosses where fatal traffic accidents had taken place. The cross would give the thinking wayfarer cause to keep the journey safe and be a little more patient as he or she drove down the road.

Imagine your life as an itinerary. List some events where the presence of His cross could have kept you more patient in a time of trial along the way of life!

You might also wish to mark your holiday calendar with crosses at the spots where you will face particularly busy times or crucial matters. This might make for a very unusual, but helpful Advent calendar.

Closing Worship

Light the third (Shepherds') candle. As you gaze into its flame, consider Jesus, the Good Shepherd, as the Light of the World. Pray, "Lord, in Your light I see light for my life and the life of all who suffer and struggle for patience. Amen."

Scripture Lessons for Next Sunday

Read in preparation for the Fourth Sunday in Advent Isaiah 7:10–14; Romans 1:1–7; and Matthew 1:18–25.

Session 4

Fourth Sunday in Advent

Isaiah 7:10–14 (15–17); Romans 1:1–7; Matthew 1:18–25

Focus

Theme: *Who's in Charge?*

Law/Gospel Focus

We desire to be the captains of our ships, the masters of our own destinies. But pushing God off the throne leaves us with a dear price to pay in terms of untold frustrations and disappointments. The Good News is that He who is always in charge provides forgiveness for our pathetic attempt at playing God. We can rejoice that He who loved us to death is indeed in charge.

Objectives

By the power of the Holy Spirit working through God's Word we will
1. confess our sinful desire to take charge of our own lives and fashion our own destiny;
2. praise God that we are the objects of His relentless love, the love of our God-with-us, Emmanuel;
3. give thanks that God has empowered us by His love to be His servants.

Opening Worship

We light the fourth "angels" candle. We meditate for a moment on these messengers of God and the role they played in the first Advent and Christmas.

Sing or speak together "Oh, Come, Oh, Come, Emmanuel" (*LW* 31).

> Oh, come, oh, come, Emmanuel,
> And ransom captive Israel,

That mourns in lonely exile here
Until the Son of God appear.

Refrain
Rejoice! Rejoice! Emmanuel
Shall come to you, O Israel!

Oh, come, our Wisdom from on high,
Who ordered all things mightily;
To us the path of knowledge show,
And teach us in her ways to go. *Refrain*

Oh, come, oh, come, our Lord of might,
Who to Your tribes on Sinai's height
In ancient times gave holy law,
In cloud and majesty and awe. *Refrain*

Oh, come, O Rod of Jesse's stem,
From ev'ry foe deliver them
That trust Your mighty pow'r to save;
Bring them in vict'ry through the grave. *Refrain*

Oh, come, O Key of David, come,
And open wide our heav'nly home;
Make safe the way that leads on high,
And close the path to misery. *Refrain*

Oh, come, our Dayspring from on high,
And cheer us by Your drawing nigh;
Disperse the gloomy clouds of night,
And death's dark shadows put to flight. *Refrain*

Oh, come, Desire of nations, bind
In one the hearts of all mankind;
Oh, bid our sad divisions cease,
And be Yourself our King of Peace. *Refrain*

Introduction

When Satan came to Eve in the Garden of Eden, he strongly implied that God did not know what was best for her and her husband. The devil's approach hasn't changed since the days of Eden. He seeks to dupe us into thinking that we can take charge of our life, going our own way without any burden of obedience to God.

1. In what areas of your life do you feel "in charge" or "in control?"

2. What areas of your life would you admit are out of your control or "out of control"?

3. How does "out of your control" sometimes become "out of control"?

4. Because of sin, God who claimed us as His own through Holy Baptism often plays no more than an extra in our lives. How does taking the control of your life from God affect your relationship with Him?

Inform

Look at each of the three lessons appointed for this Sunday. Note who the actual "doer" is in each reading.

In Isaiah 7:10–14, we meet Ahaz who was the grandson of Uzziah, the king who died in the year Isaiah saw the exalted Lord in the temple. Isaiah, acknowledging God's authority, has responded to God's question, "Who will go for us?" with the words, "Here am I. Send me!" (Isaiah 6:1–6). King Ahaz has a problem realizing that God is in charge, not the king. But *the King* calls the plays. The Lord will do the doing. He will give the sign, the sign of the virgin who will give birth to Emmanuel.

In the Epistle, Romans 1:1–7, Paul obviously knows full well who is in charge. God called him to be an apostle. God set him apart for the proclamation of the Gospel. God had given the Good News promises through the prophets long before. God sent His Son. God sent the Spirit. Through God Paul received apostleship. We belong to Jesus Christ. Grace and peace come to us through Him.

Joseph is presented to us in Matthew 1:18–25. He is a good man, a righteous man. He has formulated his plan as to what to do with pregnant Mary. But he acknowledges God's veto of his idea. "When Joseph woke up, he did what the angel of the Lord had commanded him and took Mary home as his wife. But he had no union with her until she gave birth to a son. And he gave him the name Jesus" (Matthew 1:24–25).

1. Ahaz did not want to "put the Lord to the test" by asking for a sign. What does it mean to put the Lord to the test? How was Ahaz disobedient even though he stated, "I will not put the LORD to the test"?

2. What does God share with Ahaz in spite of his disobedience?

3. What meaning do Isaiah's words have for us who also disobey God?

4. To whom does Paul give the credit for his apostleship?

5. The apostle Paul knew who was in charge. He delighted to be God's slave. But did Paul always act in accordance with this knowledge? Look at Romans 7:14–25 and discuss how it bears on this question.

6. What comfort do these verses provide to us who do not always act in accordance with God's desires for us?

7. Describe the faith of Joseph who "took Mary home as his wife." How do the events in Joseph's life and his response to these provide evidence of who was in charge of Joseph's life?

Connect

1. Have you ever demanded a sign from God? Why do people ask for signs?

2. What causes us to desire to be in charge of our lives?

3. How can our need for proof—a sign—demonstrate our desire to be in charge of our lives?

4. What wonderful comfort comes to us from knowing that God is in charge?

5. What properly motivates our surrender to God? Can we ever perfectly surrender to Him?

6. Relate the theme "who's in charge" to the message of Advent and Christmas.

Vision

During This Week

1. As you read your newspaper this week, cut out articles that depict situations of human hopelessness without God.

2. Similarly, select articles that demonstrate leadership that reflects a trust that God is in control of life and history. Don't forget to check the sports page!

3. If you are unsuccessful in completing 1 and 2 above, consider examples from your own experience with those who are confident in God's promises.

4. In your family devotions zero in on the "out of control" feelings of Mary and Joseph before God revealed His will for them.

Closing Worship

Read the Gradual for the Fourth Sunday in Advent, rejoicing in Him who is called King.

> Rejoice, greatly, O daughter of Zion!
> Shout, daughter of Jerusalem!
> See, your King comes to you,
> Righteous and having salvation.
> Blessed is He who comes in the name of the Lord.
> From the house of the Lord we bless you.

Now pray together the Collect for this Sunday.

Stir up Your power, O Lord, and come among us with great might; and because we are sorely hindered by our sins, let Your bountiful grace and mercy speedily help and deliver us; through Jesus Christ, our Lord, who lives and reigns with You and the Holy Spirit, one God, now and forever. Amen.

Scripture Lessons for Next Sunday

Read in preparation for Christmas Day, The Nativity of Our Lord, Isaiah 62:10–12; Titus 3:4–7; and Luke 2:1–20.

Session 5

The Nativity of Our Lord

Isaiah 62:10–12; Titus 3:4–7; Luke 2:1–20

Focus

Theme: *Appearances Count—They Really Do!*

Law/Gospel Focus

The very idea of Law almost seems out of place in this season of joy! We tend to overlook the burden of our sin that necessitated the humiliation (Philippians 2:5–8) of our Lord as He assumed human form. Here the Law is seen in terms of human failure that necessitated our Lord's incarnation. Law is ultimately the cause of human despair. In terms of the lessons these pictures are drawn: "Deserted;" "not because of righteous things we had done;" the coercion of Caesar; the fear of shepherds; and the callousness of Bethlehem. Indeed, much was amiss on earth, and still is!

Here Gospel is also lavished upon us. Emmanuel, God with us, provides holiness, redemption, appeal, kindness, love, salvation, grace, eternal life, and peace on earth according to these texts. What a difference the Christ makes when He dwells among us!

Objectives

By the power of the Holy Spirit working through God's Word we will
1. grapple with the despair of life without Christ;
2. rejoice over the impact of Christ's appearance for us;
3. join in proclaiming Christ to others;
4. praise God for His generosity and grace.

Opening Worship

Share fond religious memories of Christmases gone by. What name for the holy day best captures these remembrances? "Christmas" (Christ's Mass, Communion) or "The Nativity" (the historicity of Christ's birth)? Why? Perhaps the Collect of the Day hints at both. Pray it together:

> Grant, almighty God, that the birth of Your only-begotten Son in human flesh may set us free, who through sin are held in bondage; through Jesus Christ, Your Son, our Lord, who lives and reigns with You and the Holy Spirit, one God, now and forever. Amen.

Introduction

Appearances Count!

In the poverty of the Great Depression, socks and undies had to be patched or darned. What would people say of the family name if we were injured and it was discovered that we had a hole in our socks or underwear!

1. What evidence can you provide that appearances still count today?

Indeed, appearances do count. We can often tell a great deal about a person based upon his or her appearance. Unfortunately, appearances can often be deceiving.

2. How can appearances be deceiving? Give an example from your life or the life of someone you know.

3. How might Jesus' appearance on this earth be considered deceiving by some?

4. If appearances count, what might you have concluded after seeing a baby wrapped in cloths and lying in a manger?

Inform

Isaiah 62:10–12—The prophet calls for the rejuvenation of Jerusalem (Zion) and the highway that climbs to the city gates. He foretells of a festive time. The Savior brings "reward" and "recompense" for His people, who had been downcast without Him. Victory is in the air and God's people will rejoice, for their Savior comes.

Titus 3:4–7—Our Savior appeared not in wrath and judgment as we might expect. Instead, He comes in "kindness and love." He baptizes us, regenerates us (new birth), renews His Holy Spirit within us. We are generously justified and therefore, the ones who inherit life beyond time.

Luke 2:1–20—A story so familiar can dull one's theological senses. But there is much going on here beyond the simplicity of a nativity scene. On the one hand, tyrannical government brings restraints and taxation to the people. Ironically, Caesar plays into the hand of the Lord and helps fulfill the Scriptures. On the other hand, we behold the abject poverty of our Lord and His family. He is jostled in the womb of His mother forced into rushed travel. "No Vacancy" is the sign that greets the holy family. Where were Elizabeth and Zechariah, the relatives? What is this, a feedbox for a crib? A stable, given perhaps in a moment of desperate charity to a woman in labor, becomes the nursery for God incarnate! Sense the smells: beasts and bakery. Here is a frantic father and a struggling mother facing a cruel world that would not well receive the Son (John 1:11).

Much that is lowly and humble takes place here in these lowly surroundings. Angels may sing to plain shepherds, but no mention is made of such angelic song at the manger. There abides but the promise of glory to God and peace on earth.

Jabbering shepherds herald the appearance. People receive the message in awe. Mary, in that big heart of hers, treasures all that has happened.

Strangely, God is glorified in the midst of all this humiliation, which is too great for us mortals to fathom. The Savior has come in grace as well as in the powerlessness of infancy. An appearance, indeed! What you see is what you get. Unfortunately, many will not get it at all. The grace of the moment blinds eyes and hearts expecting a parade and Jerusalem reconstituted! But appearances do count. They really do. Especially this one!

The three authors (Isaiah, Paul, and Luke) of the lessons appointed for this day each created a very different picture as they were inspired by the Holy Spirit to write about the appearance of Jesus, our Lord and Savior.

1. Compare and contrast the appearance of Jesus as described by each of the authors.

2. Why do you suppose the Holy Spirit guided the authors to write such differing accounts of Jesus' appearance?

3. Which account do you find most appealing? Why?

4. Luke's account of the appearance of a Savior appeals to many people—both Christians and non-Christians. What is the reason for its wide appeal? Why might some who consider the appearance of Jesus in Luke 2:1–20 appealing also find it deceiving? See 1 Corinthians 1:18–31.

5. How might we capitalize on the appeal of Luke's account to witness to unbelievers?

6. How might you use the Epistle lesson to answer these questions about Jesus?
a. Why did God send His only Son into this world?

b. What significance does the story of Jesus' birth have for my life?

Connect

1. Contrast the first nativity scene with the celebrations of today's holiday crowds. How might we use the appeal of the first nativity to provide hope, comfort, and peace to those harried by their preparations to celebrate?

2. Are there special ways in which your church or family celebrates or can celebrate this holy day in a way that glorifies God?

3. How might the "child in us" and the "adult in us" celebrate Jesus' appearance as described in

Isaiah's account?

Paul's account?

Luke's account?

4. How could your appearance to others express the appearance of God's kindness and love in the person and work of Jesus?

Vision

During This Week

Take some quiet time in your home to reflect upon your Christmas decorations. Do they reflect the true meaning of Christmas? How might they better portray the witness of shepherds and angels? Jot down some notes for next year's celebration in your home.

What message are your children (or grandchildren or young friends) getting about Jesus, the Savior, in this season? How can you better help them zero in on the Lord's appearing?

Consider inviting a less-fotunate family to your home for a holiday meal.

Closing Worship

Sing or speak together "Gentle Mary Laid Her Child" (*LW* 57).

> Gentle Mary laid her child
> Lowly in a manger;
> There He lay, the Undefiled,
> To the world a stranger.
> Such a babe in such a place,
> Can He be the Savior?

Ask the saved of all the race
Who have found His favor.

Angels sang about His birth,
Wise Men sought and found Him;
Heaven's star shone brightly forth
Glory all around Him.
Shepherds saw the wondrous sight,
Heard the angels singing;
All the plains were lit that night,
All the hills were ringing.

Gentle Mary laid her child
Lowly in a manger;
He is still the Undefiled
But no more a stranger.
Son of God of humble birth,
Beautiful the story;
Praise His name in all the earth;
Hail the King of glory!

Scripture Lessons for Next Sunday

Read in preparation for the First Sunday after Christmas Isaiah 63:7–9; Galatians 4:4–7; and Matthew 2:13–15, 19–23.

Lesson 6

First Sunday after Christmas

Isaiah 63:7–9; Galatians 4:4–7; Matthew 2:13–15, 19–23

Focus

Theme: *Always in Jeopardy ... But Never in Jeopardy*

Law/Gospel Focus

Sin and a world ravaged by sin make us vulnerable to all kinds of dangers. We suffer from hurts that are brought about by the evil of others and—perhaps more often—are self-inflicted.

But, "when the time had fully come, God sent His Son" (Galatians 4:4). God is gracious, providing release from the clutches of sin and relief from our sin-inflicted helplessness.

Objectives

By the power of the Holy Spirit working through God's Word we will

1. identify the dangers present in this world;
2. confess our vulnerability, even as Christians, to these dangers;
3. celebrate the Good News of God's gracious intervention through Christ Jesus;
4. affirm how faith empowers us to thrive even in the face of insecurity.

Opening Worship

Read Psalm 91 responsively or in unison. Note the dangers mentioned and also the promises of God's protection.

> He who dwells in the shelter of the Most High
>   will rest in the shadow of the Almighty.
> I will say of the LORD, "He is my refuge and my fortress,
>   my God, in whom I trust."

Surely He will save you from the fowler's snare
   and from the deadly pestilence.
He will cover you with His feathers,
   and under His wings you will find refuge;
   His faithfulness will be your shield and rampart.
You will not fear the terror of the night,
   nor the arrow that flies by day,
nor the pestilence that stalks in the darkness,
   nor the plague that destroys at midday.
A thousand may fall at your side,
   ten thousand at your right hand,
   but it will not come near you.
You will only observe with your eyes
   and see the punishment of the wicked.

If you make the Most High your dwelling—
   even the LORD, who is my refuge—
then no harm will befall you,
   no disaster will come near your tent.
For He will command His angels concerning you
   to guard you in all your ways;
they will lift you up in their hands,
   so that you will not strike your foot against a stone.
You will tread upon the lion and the cobra;
   You will trample the great lion and the serpent.

"Because he loves Me," says the LORD, "I will rescue him;
   I will protect him, for he acknowledges My name.
He will call upon Me, and I will answer him;
   I will be with him in trouble,
   I will deliver him and honor him.
With long life will I satisfy him
   and show him My salvation."

Introduction

It is not unusual at times for us to consider ourselves invulnerable. Accidents, debilitating sicknesses, and other tragedies only happen to other people. But then it happens to *us*—

- Completely unannounced, an earthquake wreaks devastation, demolishing property and snuffing out lives as well.
- A hurricane, though predicted and tracked, brings destruction and death.
- An accident changes a family's entire life.
- Sudden sickness terrifies.

A healthy friend or family member dies unexpectedly—and vulnerability and mortality closes in on us.

1. Share an incident in your life that caused you to realize your vulnerability and mortality.

2. Discuss some local, national, or international tragedies that serve to emphasize the dangers and fragility of life.

3. Is life in our society filled with more dangers than existed years ago? Give reasons for your answer.

Inform

The Old Testament reading, Isaiah 63:7–9, talks about the "distress" (verse 9) of God's people. But God provides encouragement in the same verse: "In all their distress He too was distressed." God takes action on behalf of His people, motivated by His wonderful grace and compassion. "I will tell of the kindnesses of the Lord, the deeds for which He is to be praised" (verse 7a). God calls Israel His people. God assures them that He redeems them and carries them in love and mercy. We are His people today, encouraged by these same promises from God.

In the Epistle, Galatians 4:4–7, the apostle Paul refers to the birth of Jesus, the divine/human Savior, Who redeemed us from sin. He sends the Holy Spirit into our hearts, so that, as His children, we can even call Him "Daddy" ("Abba", verse 6). God loves us so dearly that He makes us His heirs.

The Holy Gospel, Matthew 2:13–15, 19–23, offers dramatic examples of God's protecting actions on behalf of His people. As we see Him watching over Joseph, Mary, and Jesus, we are made aware of the fact that God is always in control. In fact, God here uses evil human beings to fulfill His words of prophecy.

1. The "angel of His [God's] presence" proclaimed by Isaiah is certainly evidenced in the life of the holy family. What evidence do you have that the "angel of His presence" continues to save people physically and spiritually today?

2. Provide evidence from the Scriptures of God working in and through history.

3. Provide evidence from the Epistle lesson of God working in your history, life?

4. How would you respond to someone who asks, "If God works in history, why have bad things happened?" or "If God is active in the world today, why do bad things happen?"

5. How might God use the evil in this world to bring about good in the lives of His people. Provide evidence of this from your life or the life of someone you know.

6. What words from the three Scripture lessons might you share to provide comfort to someone who has recently faced a situation that has caused them to realize their vulnerability and/or mortality?

7. Summarize in a sentence or two God's message to you found in these lessons.

================== **Connect** ==================

Read the words of the hymn, "I Walk in Danger All the Way" (*LW* 391).

> I walk in danger all the way.
> The thought shall never leave me
> That Satan, who has marked his prey,
> Is plotting to deceive me.
> This foe with hidden snares
> May seize me unawares
> If I should fail to watch and pray.
> I walk in danger all the way.
>
> I pass through trials all the way,
> With sin and ills contending;
> In patience I must bear each day
> The cross of God's own sending.
> When in adversity
> I know not where to flee,
> When storms of woe my soul dismay,
> I pass through trials all the way.
>
> And death pursues me all the way,
> Nowhere I rest securely;
> He comes by night, he comes by day,
> He takes his prey most surely.
> A failing breath, and I

In death's strong grasp may lie
To face eternity today
As death pursues me all the way.

I walk with angels all the way,
They shield me and befriend me;
All Satan's pow'r is held at bay
When heav'nly hosts attend me;
They are my sure defense,
All fear and sorrow, hence!
Unharmed by foes, do what they may,
I walk with angels all the way.

I walk with Jesus all the way,
His guidance never fails me;
Within His wounds I find a stay
When Satan's pow'r assails me;
And by His footsteps led,
My path I safely tread.
No evil leads me astray;
I walk with Jesus all the way.

My walk is heav'nward all the way;
Await, my soul, the morrow,
When God's good healing shall allay
All suff'ring, sin, and sorrow.
Then, wordly pomp, begone!
To heav'n I now press on.
For all the world I would not stay;
My walk is heav'nward all the way.

1. Compare the words of this hymn to God's message to us expressed in the three lessons.

2. Underline words and/or phrases from the hymn that are especially meaningful to you. Be prepared to share these.

3. Discuss this statement, "Even though we are Christians, we are always in jeopardy … and yet never in jeopardy."

4. Was there ever a situation in your life in which you seemed to know that God was intervening? Share it, if you feel comfortable doing so.

5. Has God ever turned foreboding circumstances into positive events for you?

Vision

During This Week
Look for an opportunity this week to help and encourage someone who is going through a time of trouble or sadness. Let this person know that "relief" is spelled out in the good news that God cares and that He who can do all things is always there for us.

Closing Worship
Sing or speak together "I Walk in Danger All the Way" (*LW* 391).
Close with a few moments of silent prayer. Thank God for His loving care and ask for His continued protection.

Scripture Readings for Next Sunday
Read in preparation for the Second Sunday after Christmas Isaiah 61:10–62:3; Ephesians 1:3–6, 15–18; and John 1:1–18.

Session 7

Second Sunday after Christmas

Isaiah 61:10–62:3; Ephesians 1:3–6, 15–18; John 1:1–18

Focus

Theme: *Saying "Amen" to God*

Law/Gospel Focus

The consequences of rejecting God as Creator and Redeemer are hopelessness, fear, immorality, and sadness. God has spiritually blessed us through His only Son's life, death, and resurrection, so that we may experience the reality of His redemption, resulting in joy, hope, peace, and fulfillment.

Objectives

By the power of the Holy Spirit working through God's Word we will
1. acknowledge that God deals graciously and mercifully with us despite our unworthiness;
2. identify how God's loving actions motivate us to say "Yes!" to Him;
3. rejoice that His grace provides us opportunities to share His love.

Opening Worship

Read these words from the Introit for the day,

Great is our Lord and mighty in power; His understanding has no limit. The Lord delights in those who fear Him, who put their hope in His unfailing love. (Psalm 147:5, 11)

Then sing or speak together the first stanza of "O God of God, O Light of Light" (*LW* 83).

> O God of God, O Light of light,
> O Prince of peace and King of kings;
> To You in heaven's glory bright

> The song of praise forever rings.
> To Him who shares the Father's throne,
> The Lamb once slain but raised again,
> Be all the glory He has won,
> All thanks and praise!
> Amen, amen.

Introduction

How wonderful it is when harmony is achieved! Joyous excitement follows the announcement that an accord has been reached in labor/management negotiations. Spouses breathe a sigh of relief when disagreements that jeopardized the marriage have been resolved. Peace, harmony, and progress result when we can truly say "Amen" to one another. It is especially glorious to say "Amen" to our God, who wants the very best for us, and therefore, sent His very best into the world to die on the cross for us.

1. Share an occasion when you were very happy that two people who were at odds with each other reconciled.

2. What are some factors that may hinder living in harmony with each other?

3. What does the Christmas event tell us about the extent of God's desire to make us one with Him?

4. What other events in Jesus' life dramatically underscore God's desire to bring harmony, reconciliation, between Him and us?

5. What empowers us to say "Amen" to God?

Inform

Look over the three Scripture readings for this Sunday. Then read the summaries.

In Isaiah 61:10–62:3 God's prophet exuberantly delights in what God has done for His people especially in the righteousness He will provide through the coming Messiah.

Paul directs us, in Ephesians 1:3–6, 15–18, to look back upon what God has done through the Messiah who has come. He prays that we might come to know Him better and rejoice in the hope that He provides.

The Gospel, John 1:1–18, presents Jesus as the Word, the living revelation of God. Jesus comes to a world that is so out of harmony with God that it doesn't recognize Him or acknowledge Him who participated in creation. But, all who by God's grace receive Him, say, "Amen" to Him, and enjoy life and light.

1. What word pictures does Isaiah use to describe the gracious activities of God? Which one most clearly describes for you what God has accomplished for you in Jesus Christ?

2. What expression in the Old Testament reading is synonymous with saying amen to God?

3. In what statements does the prophet indicate that God's saving work in us becomes visible to others?

4. What spiritual blessings are ours in Christ (Ephesians 1:3)? You will find others referred to in subsequent verses of the Epistle lesson.

5. Look at Ephesians 1:17. What does the "Spirit of wisdom" have to do with our saying "Amen" to God?

6. What words in John 1:1–18 indicate failure to say "Amen" to God?

7. John 1:18 says that Jesus has revealed God to us. What truths about God has Jesus made known?

Connect

1. Can you identify with Jonah, the reluctant prophet? When do you or might you find it difficult to say amen to God?

2. What, on the basis of this Sunday's lessons, motivates us to say

amen to God? How might we demonstrate our "Amen" to God?

3. What items in your church building remind you of God's reconciling work in Christ Jesus?

4. Talk about parts of the worship service through which you are motivated and enlivened to say amen to God.

5. What dark places in your life have recently been made lighter by the presence of Emmanuel?

Vision

During This Week

This week be alert to times when you say "Amen" to God, occasions when you rejoice in your harmony with Him. Also, think about situations in which you say no to God or when you fail to see His presence. You might want to chart this in a little notebook.

Keep your eyes open for evidence of how much God loves you. Note how He wants the best for you and how this motivates you to say "Amen!"

Look for opportunities to share God's reconciling love with others this week so that they may join with you and other believers in exclaiming "Amen."

Closing Worship

Pray together the collect for the Second Sunday after Christmas.

O God, our Maker and Redeemer, who wonderfully created us and in the incarnation of Your Son yet more wonderously restored our human nature, grant that we may ever be alive in Him who made Himself to be like us; through Jesus Christ, our Lord, who lives and reigns with You and the Holy Spirit, one God, now and forever. Amen.

Listen prayerfully as someone reads stanza 4 of "O God of God, O Light of Light" (*LW* 83).

> Then raise to Christ a mighty song,
> And shout His name, His glories tell!
> Sing, heav'nly host, Your praise prolong,
> And all on earth, Your anthem swell!
> All hail, O Lamb for sinners slain!
> Forever let the song ascend!
> All hail, O Lamb enthroned to reign!
> All hail, all hail! Amen, amen.

Scripture Lessons for Next Sunday

Read in preparation for the Epiphany of Our Lord Isaiah 60:1–6; Ephesians 3:2–12; and Matthew 2:1–12.

Session 8

The Epiphany of Our Lord

Isaiah 60:1–6; Ephesians 3:2–12; Matthew 2:1–12

Focus

Theme: *What's the Big Attraction?*

Law/Gospel Focus

The overpowering darkness of sin keeps people from experiencing the love of God revealed in Jesus Christ. The Good News is that light has come into this world through the person and work of Jesus. His sacrificial death on the cross motivates and empowers believers to let His light shine through them so that those still living in darkness may walk in His light.

Objectives

By the power of the Holy Spirit working through God's Word we will
1. identify the source and impact of darkness in this world;
2. describe how Jesus shines brightly through the darkness providing those covered in darkness with the blessings of forgiveness of sins and eternal life;
3. identify ways in which Jesus shines through us providing light to those living in darkness;
4. praise God for Jesus who conquered the darkness of sin so that we may walk in His light.

Opening Worship

Read Psalm 72:15–19. Encourage class members to read each verse thoughtfully keeping this Epiphany theme in mind: May Jesus be the great attraction for all people throughout the world. Close with the Prayer of the Day:

> O God, by the leading of a star You once made known to all nations Your only-begotten Son; now lead us, who know You by

> faith, to know in heaven the fullness of Your divine goodness; through Jesus Christ, our Lord, who lives and reigns with You and the Holy Spirit, one God, now and forever. Amen.

Introduction

Is the church attractive to the world? We build beautiful buildings, advertise, develop meaningful programs, evangelize. But people are often slow in coming. Believers can scarcely imagine a life without church, the coming together of God's people. At times it seems that outsiders rarely, if ever, come. We may become discouraged at times. The great hope and promise of Epiphany is that as the Holy Spirit works in our lives through Word and Sacrament to strengthen our faith. Jesus' love shines brightly in and through us so that others may come to know Him as their Lord and Savior. Motivated by God's love for us in Jesus we desire to do that which Jesus commands, "Let your light so shine before men, that they may see your good deeds and praise your Father in heaven" (Matthew 5:16).

1. What is responsible for the church's loss of appeal to many?

2. Who makes the church a big attraction—God or us?

3. What can you and your congregation do to let Jesus' light shine brightly through you to your community? your country? the world?

Inform

Epiphany is a Greek word written in English letters. In the Scriptures, it is used only twice in the active sense of the word, literally, "to shine upon." Thus, this season is a time of enlightenment and revelation particularly as to the nature of Jesus and the nature of His people, the church. The term is not used in the lessons for this day, but is seen in a common Christmas lesson (Titus 2:11) where it is usually rendered "appeared."

Isaiah 60:1–6—The prophet foresees the ultimate glory of Zion, the habitation of the people of God, throughout this entire chapter. By inspiration Isaiah anticipates an end to earth's great darkness as the glory of the Lord rises over His people. In fact, God's own are to reflect that light and people and rulers will be drawn to them as surely as a light bulb attracts moths! From afar will come sons and daughters once dispersed, but now returned for the grand celebration. Hearts aflutter with joy, the faithful will note the great change afoot: The wealth and adulation of the heathen will be directed to the praise of God. Even the god mammon, the lure of possessions for selfish greed, is no more adored. From the East will come camels, those grand ships of the desert, ladened with the treasure. And what is this? From Sheba will come gold and incense. Isaiah knows of the magi. Or is their appearance before the young Christ but a hint of all the glory that is yet to come? Indeed, there is much to ponder here in this marvelous lesson.

Ephesians 3:2–12—Three times the word *mystery* appears in our text. Again, mystery is simply a Greek word spelled out in English letters. It does not mean a puzzlement; it means, rather, "the revealing of a hidden truth." Verse 6 expresses the mystery that the nature of God's grace (the Gospel) is that the Gentiles (heathen, non-Jewish people) will be heirs with Israel and share as one body in the promise in Jesus Christ. This revelation came to Paul and the other apostles with a clarity that no previous generation had ever experienced. The fact that Paul (v. 1) is a prisoner for (or "of") Christ, caught up in suffering (v. 13), a servant (slave) of the Gospel (v. 7) and "less than the least of all God's people" (v. 8) is not a token of discouragement for those who dare to believe; on the contrary, it is a sign of how grace ultimately effects the glory of God's people.

The proclamation is to reveal through the church to rulers and authorities in high places, a Christ, rich beyond words, as the fulfillment of the eternal plan of the Creator. Through this Christ, God is at last approachable by faith. Thus, the role of the church is one of epiphany, letting the light of the glory of Christ shine before all.

Matthew 2:1–12—This is not a Christmas story, nativity scenes take heed! It is an Epiphany story—celebrated 12 days after Christmas by liturgical churches. The day commemorates a time not of the newborn Christ but of Jesus as a child approaching two years of age (v. 16). What we have here is the fulfilling, to a significant, but minute degree, of Isaiah's prophecy. There is more of the glory of Christ still pending, but here from the East (non-Jewish) comes the beginning of the acknowledgment that Christ is Lord of all. The established monarchy is distraught that a new King and new era is dawning. It rightly senses the death knell of its power and wickedness. The religious of the court find Micah 5:2 zeroing in on the birth site: Bethlehem. For devious reasons, Herod bids the Magi (likely astrologers, certainly wisemen) to report on the whereabouts of the Child once they have located Him. "Having been warned in a dream," they will nobly and courageously refrain from doing this. Guided by the star, they reach the house (no longer a manger) where Jesus the Christ dwells with Mary and Joseph. They bow down, worship, adore, and present gifts: gold, pure incense, and myrrh (a sweet smelling desert herb or its resin prized as perfume and deodorizer; last given to Christ [Mark 16:1] at His burial). Again we have an Epiphany: The Light is dawning. God's plan becomes clearer and clearer. God brings in a broader audience to hear and to know the Truth.

1. In what sense is Matthew's account only the tip of the iceberg in the fulfillment of Isaiah's prophecy?

2. The Gospel is a mystery, a hidden truth to be revealed. What is hidden about the Gospel? How is it revealed?

3. Review the meaning of the word *epiphany*. What is the role of us whom the light of the Gospel, the Good News of Jesus has shined upon?

4. What is the significance of the fact that the Magi were not Jewish?

5. Why did Herod and his religious scholars resist the shining forth of the Christ?

6. Why do people today resist the Gospel? How do all three lessons give us hope in the wake of resistance?

Connect

1. We live in a society where the church appears to be losing ground. Many count Christianity as just another irrelevant religion. Many ridicule its precepts for life. People resist or ignore the Gospel message. Have situations like these discouraged you in your faith-life journey? What message of hope do you personally find in the Epiphany Scripture lessons?

2. As a holiday, Christmas seems to end suddenly with the opening of the last gift. What do you think of the celebrations in other cultures that last 12 days, reaching a climax on Epiphany?

3. When the author was a young pastor in the Midwest, "church" was the only real place of action in town ... and just about everyone participated or felt guilty if he or she didn't. Today there is a lot of competition for peoples' time. Considering these factors, what can we do so that the light of God's love might shine upon and be received by more people?

4. Do you expect that the church will become the "big attraction" once more in this life—or do we wait for a heavenly fulfillment of Isaiah's promise? What's the danger for us as Christians if we adopt a "sit back and wait" attitude for the fulfillment of Isaiah's promise?

5. In what ways might God use you as an Epiphany to shine upon someone you know the love of Christ Jesus?

Vision

During This Week

1. To help keep Epiphany on your mind this week, try to find how many words you can make out of its letters.

2. Plan a little post-Epiphany celebration among family or friends. Use it as a time to share in the joyous hope of this season and to bring Light into the hearts of others. Be innovative and plan to report on your get-together next week in class.

3. Bring the light of Christ to a shut-in, a troubled family, a person in need, a hurting friend, a doubting loved one, etc. Remember, Epiphany doesn't say that Christmas is over; it blurts out that it has only just begun.

Closing Worship

The leader may wish to have many unlit candles set about the room. Light one, then turn out the lights to darken the room. Light an additional candle for each Epiphany word as someone reads it aloud: shine, glory, light, appears, brightness, dawn, radiant, revelation, insight, revealed, star. Have a moment of silence in the candles' glow. Close by reciting these words (Isaiah 60:5a), "You will look and be radiant, your heart will throb and swell with joy."

Scripture Lessons for Next Sunday

Read in preparation for the Baptism of Our Lord, First Sunday after the Epiphany Isaiah 42:1–7; Acts 10:34–38; and Matthew 3:13–17.

Session 9

The Baptism of Our Lord

Isaiah 42:1–7; Acts 10:34–38; Matthew 3:13–17

Focus

Theme: *Water and the Word*

Law/Gospel Focus

Our human nature is powerless to do anything righteous, but by the Word of God connected to the water in Holy Baptism the Holy Spirit creates saving faith in Jesus and empowers us to serve Him in response to Jesus' sacrificial death on the cross.

Objectives

By the power of the Holy Spirit working through God's Word we will
1. see how powerless we are to do acceptable works according to God's perfect standards;
2. rejoice that God empowers us through the means of grace—Word and Sacrament—to do good works;
3. serve God in His mission to bring the Gospel of Jesus Christ to all people.

Opening Worship

Listen carefully as someone reads "The Sacrament of Holy Baptism as the Head of the Family Should Teach It in a Simple Way to His Household" from Luther's Small Catechism. Then pray together.

Gracious Lord, we thank You for pouring out Your grace upon us through Your Word and Your Sacraments of Holy Baptism and the Lord's Supper. Grant to us receptive hearts and minds to Your means of grace. Remind us always that we are baptized into Your family of salvation and everlasting life. In Jesus' name we pray. Amen.

Introduction

Pour a glass of water from the tap. While looking at the water, ask yourself the question, "What power does water have?" Now, think for a moment about what life would be like if you couldn't draw water from the tap for a day, two days, a week, a month. Ask yourself again, "What power does water have?" Since water has the power to sustain life, how might its absence be more than simple inconvenience?

There is enormous power too in the water of Baptism. This power is not simply in the water but in the Word of God connected with the water. Martin Luther in his Small Catechism writes, "How can water do such great things? Certainly not just water, but the word of God in and with the water does these things, along with the faith which trusts this word of God in the water."

1. What great things does God work through Baptism? For help see Acts 2:38, Ephesians 5:26, Colossians 2:12 and 1 Peter 3:21.

2. Compare the power of water in everyday life with the power of water connected with God's Word in Holy Baptism in everyday life.

Inform

Read these summaries of the Scripture lessons for the The Baptism of Our Lord or The First Sunday after the Epiphany.

Isaiah 42:1–7 is the first of four prophecies in Isaiah describing the coming Messiah as a humble servant. The other three prophecies are found in Isaiah 49:1–6; 50:4–9; and 52:13–53:12.

Acts 10:34–38—Peter has just received a vision that God through Christ accepts all people, not only Jews but also Gentiles.

Matthew 3:13–17—In His state of humiliation, Jesus is baptized by John, and the Holy Spirit descends upon Jesus.

1. Isaiah lived in the eighth century B.C. Because of the sin of the people, Israel had become a weak nation, divided into North and

South as America was in the 1860s. Northern Iraq, or Assyria, as it was called then, was a world power. What do you think was the spiritual state of the people of Israel in Isaiah's day?

2. If you were in Israel at the time of Isaiah, how might you have reacted to the words of Isaiah 42:1–7?

3. Today's Scripture lessons are for The First Sunday after the Epiphany. Epiphany is a technical term that means an eye opening event. In Acts 9 the violent man Saul's eyes were opened to see his sinful ways and to see the Lord Christ in His dazzling majesty. In Acts 10 the disciple Peter's eyes were also opened. To what did Peter have his eyes opened?

4. Through what eye-opening, sacred act, mentioned in Acts 10:37–38, does God welcome people of all races into His Kingdom?

5. At what eye-opening event is Jesus annointed by the Holy Spirit according to Acts 10:37–38? Who eventually will be blessed by Jesus' ministry?

6. Matthew 3:13–17 records what happened at Christ's Baptism. Did Jesus, true God and true man, need to be baptized? Why did Jesus go to the Jordan River to be baptized? How is Jesus' Baptism good news for us and all people?

7. What evidence of the Trinity does God reveal to us in Matthew 3:16–17?

8. How was the Trinity revealed in the words spoken at our Baptism?

Connect

1. Which of the following conditions from Isaiah 42:1–7 can you relate to at times? Choose two, and if you feel comfortable, share your choices and why.
   ____ There is no justice in life (verse 1)
   ____ I'm bruised emotionally, spiritually, or physically (verse 3)
   ____ I feel like a smoldering candle wick (verse 3)
   ____ I'm faltering (verse 4)
   ____ I'm really discouraged (verse 4)
   ____ I'm spiritually blind (verse 7)
   ____ I feel confined (verse 7)
   ____ I'm in the dark (verse 7)

2. Jesus was annointed by the Holy Spirit at His Baptism. Because of the perfect righteousness of Christ which included His death on the cross and resurrection from the dead, God also gives us the Holy Spirit at our Baptism. Go back and look at the conditions from Isaiah 42:1–7. How does our Baptism in Christ help us in each of these challenging conditions?

3. In Matthew 3:14, John the Baptist says to Jesus, "I need to be baptized by You." What did John mean?
   ____ I need to be washed by You, Christ.
   ____ I need to be forgiven of all my sins.
   ____ I need the power of the Holy Spirit that You alone can give.

____ I need to be received into Your Kingdom of believers.

For many of us as infants our parents and/or sponsors spoke for us saying, "I need to be Baptized by You." Maybe after hearing God's Word later in life the Holy Spirit led you to say, "I need to be baptized by You." What did this mean for you?

4. Acts 10:38 states that God annointed Christ with the Holy Spirit and power at His Baptism. Today there is much emphasis upon the power "within you." The declaration is "You have power in you that is just waiting to be tapped." Buddhism, Hinduism, mysticism, and the New Age philosophies teach people to look inward for enlightenment, strength, and peace. Even in the children's classic *The Wizard of Oz,* there is the idea that Oz didn't give anything to the Tin Man that he didn't already have.

In contrast to this "power within you" philosophy, what do all three Bible readings for today teach us about power? Where does true power come from?

5. Acts 10:38 states that Jesus was annointed with the Holy Spirit and power at His Baptism. Because of Christ, you are also annointed with the Holy Spirit and power at your Baptism. How could you use this God-given power to serve Him? Choose two of the following, and if you are so moved, share with the class the reason for your choices. Through my Baptism in Christ, God's power is moving me to

____ fight off the power of the devil (Acts 10:38);

____ be more consistent in daily Bible reading and devotions;

____ pray for the salvation of a friend or relative;

____ call, visit, or send a card to a "bruised reed;"

____ fight depression;

____ find comfort in the forgiveness of Christ;

____ squelch self-destructive habits;

____ stop putting things off until the last minute;

____ spend more time with my children and spouse;
____ serve Christ by volunteering at church;
____ other_____;
____ other_____.

Vision

During This Week

1. Pray for a friend or relative who is in need of God's power to trust in Christ for strength and salvation.
2. Write or call a family member or friend with a word of encouragement through Christ.
3. Read the sections on Baptism in Luther's Small Catechism.

Closing Worship

Sing or pray together the following stanzas of "All Who Believe and Are Baptized" (*LW* 225).

> All who believe and are baptized
> Shall see the Lord's salvation;
> Baptized into the death of Christ,
> They are a new creation;
> Through Christ's redemption they will stand
> Among the glorious heav'nly band
> Of ev'ry tribe and nation.
>
> With one accord, O God, we pray,
> Grant us Your Holy Spirit;
> Help us in our infirmity
> Through Jesus' blood and merit;
> Grant us to grow in grace each day
> By holy Baptism that we may
> Eternal life inherit.

Scripture Lessons for Next Sunday

Read in preparation for the Second Sunday after the Epiphany Isaiah 49:1–6; 1 Corinthians 1:1–9; and John 1:29–41.

Session 10

Second Sunday after the Epiphany

Isaiah 49:1–6; 1 Corinthians 1:1–9; John 1:29–41

Focus

Theme: *Called Instead of Condemned*

Law/Gospel Focus

Because we break God's commandments every day, we deserve to be cast from the presence of God forever. Yet God in His mercy called His Son Jesus Christ to pay the penalty for our sin. For the sake of Christ, God now calls us to serve in His Kingdom of grace.

Objectives

By the power of the Holy Spirit working through God's Word we will
1. confess that we break God's commandments every day;
2. affirm that through His death on the cross Jesus has paid the price for all of our sins;
3. marvel that instead of casting us away from Him, God calls us to serve Him in His Kingdom of grace because of Christ's sacrifice on the cross;
4. serve Christ with appreciation of the privilege He has given us to work in His Kingdom.

Opening Worship

Follow along as someone reads the words of the Third Article of the Apostles' Creed and Martin Luther's explanation of it.

I believe in the Holy Spirit; the holy Christian church, the communion of saints; the forgiveness of sins; the resurrection of the body; and the life everlasting. Amen.

> *What does this mean?* I believe that I cannot by my own reason or strength believe in Jesus Christ, my Lord, or come to Him; but the Holy Spirit has called me by the Gospel, enlightened me with His gifts, sanctified and kept me in the true faith
>
> In the same way He calls, gathers, enlightens, and sanctifies the whole Christian church on earth, and keeps it with Jesus Christ in the one true faith.
>
> In this Christian church He daily and richly forgives all my sins and the sins of all believers.
>
> On the Last Day, He will raise me and all the dead, and give eternal life to me and all believers in Christ.
>
> This is most certainly true.
>
> Pray together:
>
> Dear Father in heaven, we confess that we disobey Your commandments every day and deserve to be cast away from Your presence. We thank You for Your mercy in not only keeping us in Your Kingdom but also for calling us to the marvelous privilege of serving You to share the Gospel of Christ to all around us. For the sake of Your Son Jesus Christ, enlighten us with gratitude to Your wonderous grace. In Christ's name we pray. Amen.

Introduction

Senior citizens at Emmanuel in Gowanda, New York, support their church's elementary school even though many no longer have children or grandchildren of their own at the school. A farmer at Good Shepherd in Collinsville, Illinois, donates produce to the needy. The congregation at Lynch Emmanuel in Glenburn, North Dakota, sends cards to persons all over the world for whom prayer requests have been submitted. The members of First Lutheran Church in Dinuba, California, help to sponsor a missionary in Panama.

1. What do these persons from different parts of the U.S. have in common?

2. True or False. If false, explain why.
a._____ The work of the persons mentioned above is not as important

as the work of a president, governor, or prime minister.
b._____ Every Christian is called by God to serve because of the work of Jesus Christ on the cross.
c._____ Every Christian has a purpose on this earth.
d._____ Unless we pitch in and help God, He will never be able to get all the work He wants done on earth.
e._____ God could have chosen any number of ways to carry out His work on earth, but out of mercy He gives us the privilege of serving in His work.
f._____ We are worthy to be called into service in God's Kingdom.
g._____ It is purely out of God's grace for the sake of Jesus Christ that God calls us to serve in His body of believers.

Inform

Read the following summaries of the Scripture lessons for the Second Sunday after the Epiphany.

Isaiah 49:1–6—This section of Isaiah is the second of four prophecies known as the servant songs describing the coming Messiah who is King but also Servant. Last Sunday's reading from Isaiah 42:1–7 was the first song which emphasized the servant Christ's gentleness and mercy. Today's reading describes the servant Messiah's call long before His birth. It further declares that His mission will be to rescue the people of Israel and to reach out to save the whole world. Unless specified otherwise, the I's, Me's, and My's in the verses refer to Jesus, the servant Messiah.

1 Corinthians 1:1–9—St. Paul is in Ephesus, Turkey, when he hears disturbing reports of divisions, disobedience, and distortion of doctrine in the church of Corinth, Greece. Out of concern, he writes a letter. He begins his letter by reminding the Corinthians that God has called them into fellowship with Christ. Paul hopes that this Gospel message will motivate the Christians to respond to God's grace and amend their destructive ways.

John 1:29–41—John the Baptizer had credibility. His endorsement counted in the minds of the people. In this reading, John the Baptizer testifies that Jesus is the Son of God. John also does not object to Jesus calling his disciples to serve the Christ. One of John's disciples, Andrew, is called by Christ. Andrew then calls his brother Simon Peter to serve the Messiah.

All three lessons focus on God's call to serve. In the Old Testament reading, God calls His Son to save both Israelite and Gentile. In the Epistle, God calls all Christians to serve. In the Gospel, Jesus calls Andrew, and then Andrew calls Peter to follow the Son of God.

1. Fill in the chart based upon each of the three readings:

Scripture	Person(s) Called	Purpose(s) for Being Called
Isaiah 49:1–6		
1 Corinthians 1:1–9		
John 1:29–41		

2. Read Matthew 28:16–20. These verses have been called "The Great Commission." Read Isaiah 49:6. Why has this verse been called "The Great Commission of the Old Testament"?

3. The first part of Isaiah 49:4 describes the servant Messiah's emotions. In the second part of the verse, what gives the Messiah encouragement?

4. How many times is the word *called* used in 1 Corinthians 1:1–9? Describe in your own words its meaning.

5. Since God has called you too, what does He promise you in 1 Corinthians 1:8?

6. What was Christ called to do? See John 1:29.

7. When Jesus said, "Come," to Andrew in John 1:39, what did Andrew do? After Andrew spent a day with Christ, what did Andrew do (verse 41)?

Connect

1. Read again Isaiah 49:4. In the first part of that verse, Christ in His human nature says that His efforts were in vain. Each of the following persons were called by God's grace into faith in Jesus Christ. They all served the Lord in responding to tasks which the Lord had placed before them. Which of these situations can you relate to? Can you think of times when your efforts seemed in vain?

____ Martha feels like a failure as a parent because her adult children don't attend church anymore.

____ Ramon gave his best years to the company where he was employed, but last month he was laid off.

____ Jolene helped her friends and relatives when they were in bad shape, but now they don't even remember the sacrifices she made.

____ Ming invited her friends and relatives to church and even shared with them the Gospel, but no one has ever responded.

____ Tyrone volunteered for a church project and put in a lot of time in the evenings and on weekends, but all he got from some church members were complaints and criticism.

____ Other _____

____ Other _____

2. Read Isaiah 49:4 once more. How do we know that Christ understands how Martha, Ramon, Jolene, Ming, Tyrone, and we feel when all our efforts seem wasted?

3. Focus upon the second half of Isaiah 49:4 where the servant Messiah affirms that God the Father knows His efforts and God is the only person who matters. How does the second part of Isaiah 49:4 give hope and encouragement to the persons mentioned above?

4. In 1 Corinthians 1:1–9, Paul emphasizes how his mission and the mission of other Christians were not of his or other's design. They were called by God to the service they rendered. How does this affirmation of God's call give Paul and us encouragement when there seem to be obstacles and resistance in almost everything we do?

5. If your church is like most Christian churches, you will find that a vast majority of members join the church because a friend or relative invited them. How do we see this process in John 1:40–41? What encouragement do these verses give you as you witness to family members and friends? Can you find other encouraging verses from the other lessons?

Vision

During This Week

1. Keep a journal of frustrations you encounter, verses from the Bible that give you strength, and prayers of praise and petition.
2. Think of a Christian you know who seems to have composure when things around him or her are going haywire. Speak to that person and ask how he or she finds peace in disturbing circumstances.
3. Telephone, visit, or write one person who needs to know that Christ loves him or her.

Closing Worship

Pray together the following:

> Lord, heavenly Father, we confess that we daily break Your commandments. We deserve to be cast from Your presence. Create faith in us to trust in the forgiveness Christ purchased for us.

Grant to us a sense of awe and gladness that instead of casting us from Your presence, You have called us to serve in Your Kingdom of grace. Empower us to carry out the tasks You give us. For Jesus' sake we pray. Amen.

Scripture Lessons for Next Sunday

Read in preparation for the Third Sunday after the Epiphany Isaiah 9:1–4; 1 Corinthians 1:10–17; and Matthew 4:12–23.

Session 11

Third Sunday after the Epiphany

Isaiah 9:1–4; 1 Corinthians 1:10–17; Matthew 4:12–23

Focus

Theme: *The Gloom of Darkness, the Joy of Light*

Law/Gospel Focus

Sin has brought spiritual darkness into this world. Our compassionate God sends the light of His grace, His Son Jesus Christ, to break the darkness of sin and despair. The light of Christ gives eternal life and joy.

Objectives

By the miraculous power of the Holy Spirit through God's Word we will
1. admit that we live in spiritual darkness and disobey God's commandments and this disobedience brings darkness into our life and the lives of others;
2. celebrate during Ephipany and all throughout the year how God sent the Light of the world, Jesus Christ, to destroy the darkness of sin;
3. follow God's commandments because the Light of the world, Jesus' light, shines in our souls and upon our path.

Opening Worship

Pray together from John 1:1, 4–5, 9.
Leader: In the beginning was the Word,
Participants: and the Word was with God, and the Word was God.
Leader: In Him was life,
Participants: and that life was the light of men.
Leader: The light shines in darkness,
Participants: but the darkness has not understood it.
Leader: The true light that gives light to every man
Participants: was coming into the world. Amen.

Introduction

Have you ever experienced complete darkness? Maybe you were camping on a moonless night in a dense forest in Michigan or Oregon. Maybe you took a tour through a cave like the Meramec Caverns in Missouri. Or maybe as a child, you and your little brother or sister just hid in the closet and closed the door.

Total darkness and its effects create an overpowering feeling. You can almost feel darkness press against your skin and hum in your ear. If you're with a tour group in a cavern or sitting in a room and not needing to move, the darkness is fun. But if you are alone without a flashlight and groping in the forest or fumbling around in a strange room trying to find a light switch, darkness is not fun at all. It is a helpless, humbling feeling.

In today's Old Testament lesson and Gospel lesson, we read about people walking and living in prolonged spiritual darkness. They were in darkness because they disobeyed God. Some of the people were also in darkness because they were oppressed with the gloom of guilt for the wrong they had done.

God's grace shines through darkness. God sends His only Son, Jesus Christ, to shatter the spiritual darkness that covers the world. This spiritual darkness is the dismal cloud of sin, death, guilt, despair, and fear in the world.

1. When is total darkness fun? When is it not fun? Describe some situations in which total darkness is not fun.

2. Even if the sun is shining or the fluorescent lights are glaring brightly on us, there are times when we feel a darkness overcome us. Describe situations where darkness seemed to overcome you or someone you know.

3. Complete the following sentences. Jesus is like light because
a. He brightens_____
b. He brings warmth to_____
c. He takes away the darkness of_____
d. He enables me to see_____

Inform

Read the following summaries of the Scripture lessons for the Third Sunday after the Epiphany.

Isaiah 9:1–4—To this day, some Jews believe that the Messiah will begin his ministry in northern Israel near the area of Lake Galilee where the tribes of Zebulun and Naphtali are located.

Jesus Christ began His ministry in these areas to fulfill this prophecy from Isaiah 9. Zebulun and Naphtali were "humbled in the past" (verse 1) when superpowers from the north like Assyria and Babylon plundered these tribes before proceeding southward toward the other districts. God in His mercy sent His Son to bring light first to these districts that suffered severly in the past.

1 Corinthians 1:10–17—Paul is on the west coast of Turkey in the city of Ephesus. He hears reports of quarrels and false teaching from the congregation he served in Corinth, Greece. He writes a letter to address these problems. In this section of his letter, Paul emphasizes that God did not send him to Corinth to organize a personality cult. Rather Paul states that God sent him "to preach the Gospel" which has wisdom and power (verse 17).

Matthew 4:12–23—Jesus fulfills the words of Isaiah 9:1–4 when he begins his ministry in northern Israel in the area of Zebulun and Naphtali. His ministry of light includes preaching, teaching, healing, and making disciples.

1. Look at an Old Testament map of the 12 tribes of Israel. Find Zebulun and Naphtali. Notice where they are in relation to the Sea of Galilee. This is the area where the light of salvation would dawn (Isaiah 9:2, Matthew 4:16). Why is it significant that Jesus began his ministry in Galilee in northern Israel even though he was born in Bethlehem in southern Israel?

2. In 1 Corinthians 1:17 Paul said that his first priority was to preach the Gospel. How is the Gospel the light described in Isaiah 9?

3. In 1 Corinthians 1:10–13, Paul mentions divisions and quarrels among the Christians in Corinth. In what ways is strife or bitterness like darkness? Summarize in your own words Paul's argument.

4. When the people of Israel heard or read about darkness and light in Isaiah 9:2, they probably thought of darkness in terms of their bleak and powerless political status. Many thought of light as political emancipation from the foreign nations that dominated them. In Matthew 4:12–23, how does Jesus fulfill Isaiah 9:2 in a much deeper way than merely political liberation?

Connect

1. Contrast some of the qualities of darkness with the qualities of light.

Darkness: Light

gloom:_____

despair:_____

sadness:_____

uncertainty:_____

insecurity:_____

2. In Matthew 4:18–22, Jesus calls His first disciples who will bear witness that the Light of the World has come. Discuss the following true/false statements.

a. _____ A person who catches fish for a living is less important than a missionary.

b. _____ Jesus is calling all of us to leave our careers or our responsibilites at home to become full-time church workers.

c. _____ Jesus calls people to serve in many ways.

d. _____ Jesus calls some people to leave their jobs or their homes, and He calls others to remain where they are to serve Him.

e. _____ The Holy Spirit will guide us as to when Jesus is calling us to leave or to stay to serve Him.

3. Think about what occurs when we are in physical darkness. We can't see. We get lost. We bump into sharp or hard objects. We imagine all kinds of danger around us. We get frustrated. We trip and fall.

When we are in spiritual darkness we also struggle with similar actions. Complete the following statements to describe how Christ, the Light of the world, rescues us in our spiritual darkness.

a. He enables me to see_____
b. He guides me so I won't lose my way to_____
c. He points out dangerous objects such as_____
d. He exposes fears that weren't as gigantic and huge as I
_____

Vision

During This Week

1. Pray for someone who is experiencing spiritual darkness.
2. Make a list of those items which cause despair in your life. Pray for Christ's light to shine on each of those situations.
3. Call, visit, or write at least one person this week who needs the light of God's grace that comes through His Word.

Closing Worship

Sing or read aloud together stanza 3 of "Savior, Again to Your Dear Name" (*LW* 221).

> Grant us Your peace, Lord, through the coming night;
> For us transform its darkness into light.
> Keep us from harm and danger till the dawn;
> Your evening presence promise to Your own.

Scripture Lessons for Next Sunday

Read in preparation for the Fourth Sunday after the Epiphany Micah 6:1–8; 1 Corinthians 1:26–31; and Matthew 5:1–12.

Session 12

Fourth Sunday after the Epiphany

Micah 6:1–8; 1 Corinthians 1:26–31; Matthew 5:1–12

Focus

Theme: *God Creates a Humble Heart*

Law/Gospel Focus

Our sinful human nature deludes us into thinking that we are masters of our destiny. God in His mercy rescues us from this delusion. He sent His Son, Jesus Christ, who died for all our sins including the times when we turn away from Him and attempt to go it alone. Christ then sends the Holy Spirit who opens our eyes to see God as the only One who has control over our lives. The Holy Spirit humbles us, and we realize that God is the merciful master of our life. The Holy Spirit thus moves us to serve God and receive true fulfillment.

Objectives

By the power of the Holy Spirit working through God's Word we will

1. confess that we often turn away from God and delude ourselves into thinking that we control our own destiny;
2. acknowledge that Christ forgives our sins including the sin of excluding God from our lives;
3. rejoice that God humbles us so that we find fulfillment in serving Him.

Opening Worship

Pray together responsively the litany from Matthew 5:3–5, 11–12.

Leader: Blessed are the poor in spirit,
Participants: for theirs is the kingdom of heaven.
Leader: Blessed are those who mourn,

> Participants: for they will be comforted.
> Leader: Blessed are the meek,
> Participants: for they will inherit the earth.
> Leader: Blessed are you when people insult you, persecute you and falsely say all kinds of evil against you because of [Christ],
> All: Rejoice and be glad, because great is your reward in heaven [by the merit of Jesus Christ. In His name we pray. Amen].

Introduction

We admire people who are self-reliant. We frown upon those who can't support themselves or have to depend upon others. We live by the mottos "paddle your own canoe," "pay your own way," or "God helps those who help themselves." There's a satisfaction in being able to say, "I'm my own boss"; "I've made it on my own"; "I don't owe anybody anything"; "I do things my way"; "Nobody tells me what to do"; and "I call all the shots around here." The hero is often the self-made man or woman who has climbed the ladder of success.

The Bible, however, declares that success and fulfillment are related to the qualities that Christ had—humility and service. Since we cannot generate humility and service that are acceptable to God, Christ by His death on the cross sends us the Holy Spirit. The Holy Spirit then creates humility in us so that we will live a life of service to God where there is true fulfillment.

1. What are the dangers of believing that we control our own destiny?

2. Based upon what the Bible says, evaluate the statement "God helps those who help themselves."

3. How do many people describe a successful person? Compare or contrast these qualities with humility and service.

4. Since we cannot produce humility and service that is acceptable to God, how did God come to our rescue?

Inform

Look at the following summaries of the Scripture lessons for the Fourth Sunday after the Epiphany.

Micah 6:1–8—Like a prosecuting attorney, God brings charges against His people who have not acted justly, loved mercy, and walked humbly with Him. God reminds those who have turned from Him of His rescue, redemption, and goodness.

1 Corinthians 1:26–31—In response to the critics who arrogantly call the message of the cross foolish, Paul states how God often chooses what the world considers lowly to reveal His wisdom, power, and grace.

Matthew 5:1–12—In contrast to the conventional wisdom of the world, Jesus teaches His followers what it means to be truly blessed.

1. What did God do out of mercy and love for the people of Israel (Micah 6:4)? How does this act of mercy diffuse any arrogance that the people may have had?

2. How did the people attempt to please the Lord in Micah 6:6–7? If I believed that God was greatly impressed by all the burnt offerings I made, why might I become boastful? Why might I also become brazen and careless in my actions? What did God really want His people to do (Micah 6:8)? Who gives us the motivation to do what God requires? See Jeremiah 24:7.

3. Describe the people whom the Lord called to salvation and to service in Corinth? See 1 Corinthians 1:26. In verse 28, what is God's purpose for choosing the so-called lowly in the world? What event does the world consider foolish? See 1 Corinthians 1:18.

4. How does 1 Corinthians 1:30 diffuse any boasting on our part? How is 1 Corinthians 1:29 related to Micah 6:8?

5. The "poor in spirit" (Matthew 5:3) are not those who lack spirituality. Instead, the poor in spirit possess rich spirituality. They are humble in spirit. They recognize their sin and the severe consequences of their sin. "Theirs is the kingdom of heaven" means that those who possess saving faith will receive heaven, not because of their action, but because of their complete reliance upon God. Heaven is always a gift of pure grace, not based on what we deserve. See Ephesians 2:8–9. Describe the words and actions of those who are "poor in spirit." How are their words and actions different than someone who has walked away from God to take control of his or her life?

6. "Meek" (Matthew 5:5) does not mean timid or afraid. Meek means humble and reverent, not disrespectful toward God. Explain how a "meek" person as described by Jesus can be brave and courageous.

7. What does Matthew 5:1–12 (especially vv. 3–5) have in common with Micah 6:8 and 1 Corinthians 1:28–29?

Connect

1. In Micah 6:4–5, God reminds the people of Israel how He kept rescuing and protecting them during their journey from Egypt to the Promised Land. List some events in your life when God came to your rescue and enabled you to endure an ordeal.

How do the events you described keep you from becoming proud or arrogant?

2. 1 Corinthians 1:26–31 speaks about God humbling the rich and famous so that no one can boast of their self-achievement or status. Mark the following statements as true or false:
a. _____ God doesn't like people who are wise, influential, or rich.
b. _____ All people, rich or poor, educated or not, need humility in order to be more receptive to God's grace in Christ Jesus.
c. _____ We can generate our own humility.
d. _____ Christ is our wisdom from God (v. 30).
e. _____ Christ is our righteousness, holiness, and redemption (v. 30).
f. _____ A proper kind of boasting is where God gets all the glory and credit (v. 31).

3. When I have lost my job, suffered a heart attack, or am way behind in my work, I don't feel blessed. On the contrary, I feel distressed, compressed, or depressed. Look at Matthew 5:1–12. What factors make me still blessed in spite of how I feel or how my life is going?

4. Write a list of how the world defines *blessed*. Compare and contrast this list with the list Jesus gives in Matthew 5:1–12.

Vision

During This Week

1. Each day take one verse of Jesus' Beatitudes (Matthew 5:3–12) and reflect upon it as you answer these questions: Who are the people to whom Jesus is referring? How am I like these people? What is the promise Christ makes?

2. Write the names of people who are being blessed in the ways described by Jesus in Matthew 5:3–12. Pray that God would give them strength and continue to give them the awareness that they are truly being blessed by God.

Closing Worship

Pray together the petition "For Likeness to Christ" from *LW*, page 125.

> O God, by the patient suffering of Your only-begotten Son You have beaten down the pride of the old enemy. Now help us, we humbly pray, rightly to treasure in our hearts all that our Lord has of His goodness borne for our sake that after His example we may bear with patience all that is adverse to us; through Jesus Christ, our Lord. Amen.

Scripture Lessons for Next Sunday

Read in preparation for the Fifth Sunday after the Epiphany Isaiah 58:5–9a, 1 Corinthians 2:1–5, and Matthew 5:13–20.

Session 13

Fifth Sunday after the Epiphany

Isaiah 58:5–9a; 1 Corinthians 2:1–5; Matthew 5:13–20

Focus

Theme: *Living the Faith*

Law/Gospel Focus

Sometimes we fool ourselves into thinking that we can make ourselves right with God by doing a good and moral act. However, because God's Law demands perfection, we can never make ourselves right with God and cannot fulfill His Law. He, therefore, sent His only Son, Jesus Christ, who lived the perfect life that we would never be able to live. By Christ's sacrificial death on the cross, Jesus transfers His record of perfection and puts it on our account so that God looks upon us as righteous.

Objectives

By the power of the Holy Spirit working through God's Word we will
1. admit that at times we lull ourselves into thinking that by going to church or doing some good act we have made ourselves right with God;
2. thank God that through His Law He makes us aware of this misconception;
3. declare our total dependence upon Christ because we cannot live the perfect life of obedience that God requires;
4. praise God because the perfect life of Jesus and His blood shed on the cross at Calvary cover our imperfection and God looks upon us as righteous.

Opening Worship

Sing or speak together "Take My Life, O Lord, Renew" (*LW* 404).

Take my life, O Lord, renew,
Consecrate my heart to You;
Take my moments and my days;
Let them sing Your ceaseless praise.

Take my hands and let them do
Works that show my love for You;
Take my feet and lead their way,
Never let them go astray.

Take my voice and let me sing
Praises to my Savior King;
Take my lips and keep them true,
Filled with messages from You.

Take my silver and my gold,
All is Yours a thousandfold;
Take my intellect, and use
Ev'ry pow'r as You shall choose.

Make my will Your holy shrine,
It shall be no longer mine.
Take my heart, it is Your own;
It shall be Your royal throne.

Take my love; my Lord, I pour
At Your feet its treasure store;
Take my self, Lord, let me be
Yours alone eternally.

Introduction

 We are people with checklists. Even if we don't carry around a day planner or a "Things to Do Today" scratch pad, we keep a checklist in our head. Wash the car—check. Buy groceries—check. Drive Aaron to soccer—check. At times we even think of worship as something on our list to check off. We may also think of acts of kindness during the week as something to check off, something we are done with.

 1. How do you feel when you've just checked off as "done" a chore on your "Things to Do Today" list?

2. What is the danger of looking upon worship as just another thing to do in my busy schedule?

3. How can checklists get you down and make you feel guilty? How can checklists make you feel proud?

4. Are checklists bad? What is the value of having a checklist?

5. What is the danger of looking upon God's commandments as a checklist? How are the Ten Commandments different from a checklist?

Inform

Read the following summaries of the Scripture lessons for the Fifth Sunday after the Epiphany.

Isaiah 58:5–9a—The people of Israel ask God why so much calamity has stricken them even though they have fasted religiously. God reminds them that their fasting is useless because they have neglected compassion and mercy.

1 Corinthians 2:1–5—St. Paul emphasizes that our faith depends not upon human resources but upon the power of the Holy Spirit who points to Jesus Christ and Him crucified.

Matthew 5:13–20—Jesus implies that it is impossible to keep all the commandments according to God's standards of perfection. Hence, salvation comes only by the grace of God through His Son who fulfilled perfectly the Law.

1. What kinds of things does God consider to be a form of fasting in Isaiah 58:6–7? How are these actions like a fasting?

2. God does not forbid fasting in Isaiah 58:5–9a. What, however, does He say about fasting or any other act of worship?

3. In 1 Corinthians 2:2, Paul is aware that there is only one basic message that will change hearts, bring salvation, and motivate people to do good works. What is that one and only message?

4. 1 Corinthians 2:5 states that our faith is not dependent upon human resources such as wisdom. On what does our faith rest?

5. After hearing Jesus, people might get the impression that He was doing away with the Law and commandments. What, however, does Jesus emphasize in Matthew 5:17–18?

6. One might become discouraged after reading Matthew 5:13–20 because there appears to be so many heavy demands placed upon us— to be salt, to be light, to keep every commandment, to have higher standards than the Pharisees. Find Gospel messages in Matthew 5:13–20 or elsewhere in the Bible that give encouragement to someone who feels the burden of God's Law.

Connect

1. Sometimes we feel good after we've gone to church or done a good deed to help someone. Which of the following reasons for feeling good after doing a good work are proper (Mark with a P) and which are improper (Mark with an I) according to today's Scripture readings and elsewhere in the Bible?

a. _____ I have the great satisfaction of checking off another item on my "Things to Do Today" list for God.

b. _____ I chalked up another reward for me in heaven or maybe even here on earth.

c. _____ I thank God for the grace He has given me through His Word and Sacraments that motivate me to do good works.

d. _____ I needed to prove to myself that I'm not such a bad person after all.

2. Sometimes we elevate certain duties in the Christian life at the expense of other activities. In Isaiah 58, the people had elevated ritualistic fasting to be so significant that they had forgotten about justice and mercy. In 1 Corinthians 2, the Christians had placed such an inordinate importance on wisdom they had overlooked the Gospel of Jesus Christ. What activities do you at times emphasize at the expense of other duties?

3. In what ways are the following values in our society decaying?

The family

Honesty

The church

Entertainment

Commitment

Government

How can we by the Holy Spirit's power, be salt (a preservative) and light for these values?

4. What is the significance of Jesus' statement in Matthew 5:17 that He came to fulfill the Law? Choose from the following:
a. _____ He came to do that which we could never accomplish—keep the Law perfectly.
b. _____ He came to revise the Old Testament commandments.
c. _____ Because He lived a perfect life and offered a perfect sacrifice on the cross, God the Father accepts Christ's perfection as a payment for all our sin.
d. _____ Jesus gave a new and improved version of the Law.
How is Jesus' action on our behalf significant to our lives?

Vision

During This Week

1. Reflect upon or discuss these questions: What is the purpose of worship? What is the relationship between worship and everything else that goes on in our life?
2. During this season of Epiphany, take time to reflect upon Jesus as the Light of the world and how He in Matthew 5:14 calls us to reflect His light in our lives.
3. Talk about salt and what it means that God has called us to be salt.

Closing Worship

Sing or speak together "May We Your Precepts, Lord, Fulfill" (*LW* 389).

> May we Your precepts, Lord, fulfill
> And do on earth our Father's will
> As angels do above;

Still walk in Christ, the living way,
With all Your children and obey
The law of Christian love.

So may we join Your name to bless,
Your grace adore, Your pow'r confess,
To flee from sin and strife.
One is our calling, one our name,
The end of all our hopes the same,
A glorious crown of life.

Spirit of life, of love and peace,
Our hearts unite, our joy increase,
Your gracious help supply.
To each of us the blessing give
In Christian fellowship to live,
In joyful hope to die.

Scripture Lessons for Next Sunday

Read in preparation for the Sixth Sunday after the Epiphany Deuteronomy 30:15–20; 1 Corinthians 2:6–13; Matthew 5:20–37.

Session 14

Sixth Sunday after the Epiphany

Deuteronomy 30:15–20;
1 Corinthians 2:6–13; Matthew 5:20–37

Focus

Theme: *The Letter of the Law, the Spirit of the Law*

Law/Gospel Focus

In His love God gave His Law for our physical and spiritual protection and safety. As humans we abuse His Law by emphasizing the letter of the Law at the expense of its spirit, by emphasizing the spirit of the Law at the expense of the letter, or by rejecting both the letter and the spirit of the Law. God has mercy on us in spite of our abuse of His good and wise Law. God sends His Son, Jesus Christ, who perfectly obeys both the letter and the spirit of the Law. By His death on the cross, Christ substitutes His perfect obedience for our disobedience so that Christ's righteousness covers us.

Objectives

By the power of the Holy Spirit working through God's Word we will
1. confess that we either ignore God's Law or elevate it beyond what it is capable of performing;
2. ask the Lord to give us a proper understanding of the value and function of the Law in relation to the Gospel of Jesus Christ;
3. rejoice that Christ has fulfilled the Law perfectly and by His sacrificial death on the cross has transferred His perfect record to cover our sinful record.

Opening Worship

Sing or speak together "The Law of God Is Good and Wise" (*LW* 329).

> The Law of God is good and wise
> And sets His will before our eyes,
> Shows us the way of righteousness,
> And dooms to death when we transgress.
>
> Its light of holiness imparts
> The knowledge of our sinful hearts
> That we may see our lost estate
> And seek escape before too late.
>
> To those who help in Christ have found
> And would in works of love abound
> It shows what deeds are His delight
> And should be done as good and right.
>
> When men the offered help disdain
> And willfully in sin remain,
> Its terror in their ear resounds
> And keeps their wickedness in bounds.
>
> The Law is good; but since the fall
> Its holiness condemns us all;
> It dooms us for our sin to die
> And has no pow'r to justify.
>
> To Jesus we for refuge flee,
> Who from the curse has set us free,
> And humbly worship at His throne,
> Saved by His grace through faith alone.

Introduction

People have different attitudes toward Law. Legalists emphasize the letter of the Law and ignore the spirit or reason behind the Law. Idealists promote the spirit of the Law while disregarding the letter of the Law. Anarchists reject both the letter and the spirit of the Law.

1. What do legalists forget when they look at the Law?

2. What is the danger of the idealist's point of view that only the spirit of the Law matters?

3. Was Jesus an idealist in that He emphasized the spirit of the Law while disregarding the letter? Why or why not?

4. How do anarchists demonstrate their attitude toward the spirit and letter of the Law?

Inform

Read the summaries of the Scripture lessons for the Sixth Sunday after the Epiphany.

Deuteronomy 30:15–20—Moses reminds the people of Israel that God's commandments are given to curb lawlessness, self-destruction, and disarray; to show the people their sin; and to guide them to lead a God-pleasing life.

1 Corinthians 2:6–13—St. Paul expounds on the work of the Holy Spirit who gives understanding and teaches spiritual truths.

Matthew 5:20–37—Jesus informs His followers that the righteousness which God demands goes farther than just the letter of the Law. God demands that we follow both the letter and the spirit of the Law.

1. What is the spirit or reason for God's Law (Deuteronomy 30:16)?

2. Based upon 1 Corinthians 2:14, can we understand the spirit of the Law without the Holy Spirit teaching us? How is it that we are able to appreciate both the letter and the spirit of the Law?

3. In Matthew 5:20–37, how did the letter of the Law define murder (v. 21), adultery (v. 27), and divorce (v. 31)? Jesus certainly affirmed the letter of the Law. He also recognized the spirit of the Law. According to the spirit of the Law, how did He define murder (v. 22), adultery (v. 28), and divorce (v. 32)?

4. Since Jesus clearly demonstrates that we do not and cannot keep the letter and the spirit of the Law, is there hope for us? Read Romans 7:7–25. Paul states how we do not and cannot keep the letter and the spirit of the Law. What then is our only hope for salvation from our lost condition (vv. 24–25)?

Connect

1. Some people criticize Christianity by saying that it only beats you down with endless rules and regulations. You can never be good enough. Comment.

2. What is the significance of the statement "The LORD is your life" (Deuteronomy 30:20)?

3. We live in a lawless age. Crime, violence, the break up and break down of families cause even unbelievers of Christ to demand law and order and more morality. The public looks to the church to teach good behavior and values. What is the danger when Christians believe the church's primary role is to reform an immoral society? What opportunity does the church have in a society that desperately looks for help from its moral woes?

4. In these troubled and confused times, the public demands more law and punishment as the answer. Many church members also beg their pastors to preach more Law in their sermons. "Pastor, we need more sermons against abortion, doctor-assisted suicide, pornography, drugs and alcohol, divorce, and homosexuality." Comment on whether the Christian church has been "too soft on sin" and needs to preach more Law. Comment on the danger of going too far in the other direction of preaching too much Law at the expense of the Gospel. Reflect upon the statement "More law is the answer to the moral decline of our society."

5. Scripture teaches that only the Gospel—the Good News of Jesus' life, death, and resurrection—has the power to transform lives wrought with sin. What does this say to the Christian congregation that desires to impact their community?

Vision

During This Week

1. Reflect upon the poignancy of Moses' farewell sermon in Deuteronomy. Refer to Joshua 24:15 that echoes the Mosaic scene.
2. Evaluate the merits and dangers in the strategy of Christian churches who fight evil in society through boycotting, picketing, censorship of books in public libraries, or politically organizing to support Christian candidates.
3. Observe how the letter and spirit of the Law are broken in the events that take place in your life. Ponder upon the magnitude of God's love for you in Christ.

Closing Worship

Read together the following section from the "General Prayer of the Church" (*LW,* p. 133).

> [All mighty and all merciful, Lord,] as we are strangers and pilgrims on earth, help us by true faith and a godly life to prepare for the world to come, doing the work You have given us to do while it is day, before the night comes when no one can work. And when our last hour comes, support us by Your power, and receive us into Your heavenly kingdom; through Jesus Christ, Your Son, our Lord, who lives and reigns with You and the Holy Spirit, one God, now and forever. Amen.

Scripture Lessons for Next Sunday

Read in preparation for the Seventh Sunday after the Epiphany Leviticus 19:1–2, 17–18; 1 Corinthians 3:10–11, 16–23; and Matthew 5:38–48.

Session 15

Seventh Sunday after the Epiphany

Leviticus 19:1–2, 17–18;
1 Corinthians 3:10–11, 16–23; Matthew 5:38–48

Focus

Theme: *The Perfect Son of God*

Law/Gospel Focus

God created us in His image of holiness and perfection. Sin totally destroyed that image. God in His compassion sent His Son, Jesus Christ, to live a perfect life in accordance with the image God gave us at creation. By His sacrificial death on the cross, Christ substitutes His holiness for our sinful life. Furthermore, God sends the Holy Spirit to generate a holy response in us toward God and our fellow humans.

Objectives

By the power of the Holy Spirit working through God's Word we will
1. confess that we can never fulfill God's standards for a holy life;
2. rejoice that God sent His Son, Jesus Christ, to live the holy life that we cannot live;
3. thank God that because Christ's holiness covers us, God declares us holy;
4. affirm the work of the Holy Spirit who generates holy acts and thoughts in us.

Opening Worship

Sing or speak together "Holy, Holy, Holy" (*LW* 168).

> Holy, holy, holy, Lord God Almighty!
> Early in the morning our song shall rise to Thee.
> Holy, holy, holy, merciful and mighty!
> God in three Persons, blessed Trinity!
>
> Holy, holy, holy! All the saints adore Thee,
> Casting down their golden crowns around the glassy sea;
> Cherubim and seraphim falling down before Thee,
> Which wert and art and evermore shalt be!
>
> Holy, holy, holy! Though the darkness hide Thee,
> Though the eye made blind by sin Thy glory may not see,
> Only Thou art holy; there is none beside Thee,
> Perfect in pow'r, in love and purity.
>
> Holy, holy, holy! Lord God Almighty!
> All Thy works shall praise Thy name in earth and sky and sea.
> Holy, holy, holy, merciful and mighty!
> God in three Persons, blessed Trinity.

Introduction

In our Gospel lessson for today, Jesus says, "Be perfect, therefore, as your heavenly Father is perfect." Many psychologists and counselors today would disagree with Jesus' command to be perfect. Conventional wisdom also claims that perfectionism is the root of suicide, depression, chronic procrastination, anxiety, stress, and a host of other mental disorders. Perfectionism is based upon the perfection you attain in the things you attempt. Mental health experts say that it is unrealistic for people to be perfect, and when TV advertisements, athletic coaches, parents, and even preachers push people toward perfectionism, people eventually break down from all the pressure and unreasonable expectations.

1. Does Christ teach perfectionism? If He is not teaching perfectionism, why does He command, "Be perfect"?

2. Explain in your own words this statement: One purpose of the Law is to show us our sin so that by the power of the Holy Spirit we are receptive to the Gospel which shows us our Savior. Using this principle, complete the following sentence: One purpose of the Law is to show us that we are not perfect so that we

3. Christ's command to be perfect can be balanced with His words of comfort and encouragement when we are broken in spirit and realize that we are not perfect. Read Matthew 10:28–30. What do these verses assure us—sinners unable to "be perfect"?

Inform

Leviticus 19:1–2, 17–18—God reminds His people that since God their Creator and Protector is holy, they should reflect His holiness—in their relationship to Him and to others.

1 Corinthians 3:10–11, 16–23—Christians are God's temple and are therefore holy. The Holy Spirit lives in them.

Matthew 5:38–48—As God's people we look to Jesus for our salvation. Jesus deflates our pride by explaining how God demands holiness and perfection which includes loving our enemy.

1. In Leviticus 19:1–2 the word *holy* means to be separate from the world. In what ways are God's people to be separate from the world?

2. How is Leviticus 19:1–2 related to Genesis 1:26–27?

3. The "you" in 1 Corinthians 3:16 is plural and refers to the church, the body or people of Christ. What is the significance of Jesus living in the body of believers?

4. In 1 Corinthians 3:19, what does Paul say is foolishness in God's sight? Give examples of this kind of foolishness?

5. How is God's perfect standard higher than the letter of the Law that says "An eye for eye, and a tooth for tooth?" See Matthew 5:38–42.

Connect

1. Holy means to be separate or different from the world. How are Christians separate from the world? How can a Christian's desire to be separate from the world become sinful?

2. Using logic, some people say, "God will never command you to do anything that you cannot do." This statement sounds reasonable. The Bible, however, teaches that God according to His perfect standard does command us to do and to be what we sinful humans cannot do and be. See Matthew 5:48 and Romans 3:9–12. How does our merciful God still make it possible for us to be saved? See Hebrews 7:26–28.

3. Both Leviticus 19:1–2, 17–18 and Matthew 5:38–48 refer to holy and perfect behavior in our relationship with others. Based upon these verses and by the power of the Holy Spirit, in what God-pleasing ways could you respond to the following situations?

a. A driver has cut you off on the freeway.
b. A fellow worker is telling lies about you.
c. No one in your family helps out around the house.
d. You live or work with a person who has severe mood swings.
e. A friend or relative has not paid back money you loaned him or her.

Vision

During This Week

1. Think of one person who has treated you poorly. Pray for that person. By the work of the Holy Spirit show that person at least one act of compassion for Christ's sake.

2. Read Galatians 3 that reminds us that we cannot obtain perfection and holiness by keeping the Law. Ponder especially Galatians 3:24 that declares that one purpose of the Law is to lead us to Christ.

Closing Worship

Read together the prayer "For the Holy Spirit" from page 124 of *Lutheran Worship*.

> Almighty and everlasting God, of Your great mercy in Jesus Christ You have granted us forgiveness of sin and all things pertaining to life and godliness. Therefore send us Your Holy Spirit that He may so rule our hearts that we, being ever mindful of Your fatherly mercy, may strive to overcome the world and, serving You in holiness and pureness of living, may give You continual thanks for all Your goodness; through Jesus Christ, our Lord. Amen.

Scripture Lessons for Next Sunday

Read in preparation for the Eighth Sunday after Epiphany Isaiah 49:13–18; 1 Corinthians 4:1–13; and Matthew 6:24–34.

Session 16

Eighth Sunday after the Epiphany

Isaiah 49:13–18; 1 Corinthians 4:1–13; Matthew 6:24–34

Focus

Theme: *Who Cares? God Does!*

Law/Gospel Focus

When our world seems to cave in on us, we waver in our trust that God will protect us according to His gracious and compassionate will. God forgives our sin of doubt, because Jesus Christ paid for all our sins on the cross. Christ sends us the Holy Spirit, the Comforter, who strengthens our trust in God through His encouraging Word.

Objectives

By the power of the Holy Spirit working through God's Word we will
1. confess to God our panic when things look precarious and uncertain;
2. express our joy that because of Christ's work of redemption, God forgives us when we fail to trust Him;
3. articulate with a firm conviction that God will never abandon us.

Opening Worship

Sing or speak together "I Am Trusting You, Lord Jesus" (*LW* 408).

> I am trusting You, Lord Jesus,
> Trusting only You;
> Trusting You for full salvation,
> Free and true.
>
> I am trusting You for pardon;
> At Your feet I bow,

> For Your grace and tender mercy
> Trusting now.
>
> I am trusting You for cleansing
> In the crimson flood;
> Trusting You to make me holy
> By Your blood.
>
> I am trusting You to guide me;
> You alone shall lead,
> Ev'ry day and hour supplying
> All my need.
>
> I am trusting You for power;
> You can never fail.
> Words which You Yourself shall give me
> Must prevail.
>
> I am trusting You, Lord Jesus;
> Never let me fall.
> I am trusting You forever
> And for all.

Introduction

We live in an uncertain and unpredictable world. We often fail to trust in God, our Provider and Protector. Undue worry can disintegrate our trust in God and our energy that could be used for more useful purposes. God's medicine for worry is His Word through which proclaims His care for us.

1. Mark the following as RC (Real Concern) or UC (Unsubstantiated Concern).

a. _____ Your car won't start.
b. _____ Your car won't start and your mechanic tells you that it will cost a thousand dollars to repair.
c. _____ You notice for the first time that you have a lump on your arm.
d. _____ You notice for the first time that you have a lump on your arm and you know that it will be malignant.
e. _____ You hear a rumor that your company is downsizing.
f. _____ You hear a rumor that your company is downsizing and you

are certain that you will be let go and you'll lose your house.
g. _____ You have just committed a sin.
h. _____ You have just committed a sin and you don't think God will ever forgive you.

2. What is the difference between a real concern and an unsubstantiated concern?

3. Is real concern a sin? Is unsubstantiated concern a sin? Why or why not?

We know that just saying "Don't worry" doesn't eliminate unsubstantiated concern. In fact, saying to ourselves "Don't worry" can even add to the tension and frustration as we get angry with ourselves for still worrying. Only the Holy Spirit working through the Word of God can comfort and calm, give peace and encouragement in stressful situations.

Our failure to trust in God is just one other symptom of our sinful condition. Jesus suffered and died on the cross for our sins. The love for us that led Him to the cross and the forgiveness He earned for us on the cross enable us to face stress-filled situations with renewed hope and confidence.

Inform

Isaiah 49:13–18—God promises to deliver His people from bondage. God fulfilled this promise politically when the Babylonian Captivity ended in the sixth century B.C. God has continued to fulfill this promise spiritually throughout the ages and today continues to fulfill the promise as the Holy Spirit working through God's Word and Sacrament brings people to faith in Jesus.

1 Corinthians 4:1–13—Paul describes how he and those faithful to Christ are being persecuted as the scum of the earth. Yet Paul affirms God's deliverance and victory.

Matthew 6:24–34—Jesus assures His followers that God will provide what is truly needed to all who seek first His Kingdom in which Christ rules with grace and mercy.

1. In Isaiah 49:13, why do the heavens, earth, and the mountains shout for joy?

2. Zion is a mountain or hill in Jerusalem and often represents the nation of Israel. How are the people of Zion feeling in Isaiah 49:14? Why?

3. With whom does God compare Himself in Isaiah 49:15 in order to illustrate His enduring love for His people?

4. Isaiah 49:16 says that God engraves the names of His people on the palms of His hands. This may refer to the priests carving the names of the tribes of Israel on a stone that was placed on the priests vest called the ephod (Exodus 28:9–12). How is this message a comfort to those in distress?

5. Isaiah 49:17–18 points to the return of the Israelites to the land which had been conquered by Babylon. In a spiritual way how is this return still taking place by all who trust in Christ as the Savior?

6. Why is Paul confident in spite of attacks against him (1 Corinthians 4:4–5)?

7. In 1 Corinthians 4:10–13, Paul catalogs the adversity that he and other apostles have had to endure. Why does Paul, however, still have hope and confidence? See verses 4–5.

8. What are the comforting messages of Matthew 6:26–33?

9. In Matthew 6:32–33, what is one of many differences between a pagan and a follower of Christ?

================= **Connect** =================

1. The people of Zion feel that the Lord has forsaken and forgotten them (Isaiah 49:14). When do we feel forgotten and forsaken by God? What is the encouraging message in verse 15?

2. When things are going well for a person, we sometimes hear others say, "Well, he or she must be doing something right." Based upon 1 Corinthians 4:8–13, what would St. Paul say about the attitude that things will go "well" for those who are doing things right?

3. Jesus says in Matthew 6:34, "Do not worry about tomorrow." Explain whether Jesus would agree or disagree with the following attitudes.

a. Since Jesus said not to worry about tomorrow, I think it is wrong to purchase car, house, medical or life insurance. If I get injured or if my property is damaged, God will take care of my needs and the needs of my loved ones.

b. Since Jesus said not to worry about tomorrow, I'm just going to take it easy and just get by at work. I mean why strain myself since everything is in God's hands?

c. By the power that God gives, I'm going to work hard everyday and by His grace in Christ, I am praying for His strength to fight worry.

d. Since Jesus said not to worry about tomorrow, I'm not going to make plans about my career, retirement, or anything. I'm just going to live one day at a time and not think about the future.

4. Based upon the three readings for today and upon all of Scripture, mark the following statements as True or False.
a. _____ Jesus promises that no Christian will ever be hungry, naked, or poor.
b. _____ If a Christian is hungry, naked, or poor, the Christian is still blessed with priceless spritual gifts such as forgiveness, eternal life, and peace with God.
c. _____ If you live the Christian life faithfully, you will be blessed with good income and health.

105

d. _____ No matter what our health or income is like, the believer in Christ Jesus is always blessed by God with His grace and mercy.
e. _____ For the faithful in Christ, financial and medical status may change, but Christ's love and compassion does not.

Vision

During This Week

1. List a number of your personal anxieties. Now meditate on God's great love for you demonstrated when He sent His only Son to suffer and to die on the cross to receive the punishment you deserved because of sin. By the prompting of the Holy Spirit, pray that God will strengthen faith and trust in Him for Christ's sake.

2. Analyze your prayers. Have your prayers become merely wish lists for self or a catalog of your anxieties. If so, by the work of the Holy Spirit through God's means of grace, include praise and thanksgiving for the spiritual blessings of forgiveness, mercy, peace with God, and eternal life that God has granted you.

Closing Worship

Sing or speak together "What Is the Word to Me" (*LW* 418).

> What is the world to me
> With all its vaunted pleasure
> When You, and You alone,
> Lord Jesus, are my treasure!
> You only, dearest Lord,
> My soul's delight shall be;
> You are my peace, my rest.
> What is the world to me!

> The world seeks to be praised
> And honored by the mighty
> Yet never once reflects
> That they are frail and flighty.
> But what I truly prize
> Above all things is He,
> My Jesus, He alone.
> What is the world to me!

The world seeks after wealth
And all that mammon offers
Yet never is content
Though gold should fill its coffers.
I have a higher good,
Content with it I'll be:
My Jesus is my wealth.
What is the world to me!

What is the world to me!
My Jesus is my treasure,
My life, my health, my wealth,
My friend, my love, my pleasure,
My joy, my crown, my all,
My bliss eternally.
Once more, then, I declare:
What is the world to me!

Scripture Lessons for Next Sunday

Read in preparation for the Transfiguration of Our Lord, the Last Sunday after the Epiphany Exodus 24:12, 15–18; 2 Peter 1:16–19 (20–21); Matthew 17:1–9.

Session 17

The Transfiguration of Our Lord

Exodus 24:12, 15–18; 2 Peter 1:16–19 (20–21); Matthew 17:1–9

Focus

Theme: *Christ's Majesty and Mercy*

Law/Gospel Focus

Because of sin we often take God for granted as we treat God casually in our attitude and in our actions. As the Holy Spirit moves us to confess our sins, God forgives all our sins including the sin of taking Him for granted because Jesus Christ paid the price for our sins when He suffered and died on the cross.

Objectives

By the power of the Holy Spirit working through God's Word we will
1. confess to God how we at times get casual and irreverent in our attitude toward Him;
2. affirm through the words of Scripture the magnificence and majesty of our awesome God;
3. pray with a sense of astonishment at how our powerful God uses His might in showing us His grace and mercy.

Opening Worship

Pray together selected verses from Psalm 99, the Introit for The Transfiguration of our Lord.
Leader: Exalt the Lord our God and worship at His holy mountain,
Participants: for the Lord our God is holy.
Leader: The Lord reigns,
Participants: let the nations tremble.
Leader: Let them praise Your great and awesome name—
Participants: He is holy.

> All: Glory be to the Father and to the Son and to the Holy Spirit; as it was in the beginning, is now, and will be forever. Amen.

Introduction

There are two opposite and equally wrong extremes that we may fall into when we think of God. On the one hand, we may, as young Martin Luther did, look upon Him primarily as the stern and vengeful God who breathes fire and brimstone. On the other hand, we may treat Him casually as our good buddy or as a jolly old Santa Claus who never gets angry or upset.

1. Which attitude is more prevalent today—people overly terrified of an angry, vengeful God or people taking God too casually? Explain.

2. What is wrong with churches that preach only fire and brimstone messages about God? What is wrong with churches that preach only a "happy face" God?

3. Why is it important that the church teaches God's Law—shows us our sin and God's anger over sin? God's Gospel—shows us our Savior and the forgiveness of sins because Jesus received the punishment we deserved when He suffered and died on the cross?

Inform

Read the following summaries for the three lessons of the day.
Exodus 24:12, 15–18—On Mount Sinai, the glory of the Lord looked like a consuming fire. Yet God in His mercy and grace calls

Moses up the mountain to receive the Ten Commandments.

2 Peter 1:16–19 (20–21)—Peter attests to how he was an eyewitness to the majestic glory of the Lord Christ. Yet by the kindness and mercy of God he still lives to share how every prophetic word of Scripture is true.

Matthew 17:1–9—Peter, James, and John see the transfigured Christ, shining like the sun and bright as light, and are enveloped by a bright cloud of the Lord. Yet by the gentleness and compassion of God they live and are instructed not to tell anyone until after Jesus' resurrection.

1. In Exodus 24:17, what did the glory of God look like to the Israelites? How long did Moses stay on the mountain covered by the glory of the Lord? Why wasn't Moses burnt to a crisp on the mountain?

2. In 2 Peter 1:16–19, what did Peter, James, and John see? What did they hear?

3. What was the result of events such as the transfiguration in relation to the word of the prophets (2 Peter 1:19)?

4. Who talked with the transfigured Jesus (Matthew 17:3)? God gave _____ the Law and appointed _____ to be a prophet. Hence, some Bible scholars have pointed out that Jesus here fulfills the Law and Prophets.

5. In Matthew 17:6, what does Jesus say to the disciples who are terrified? What do Jesus' words and actions toward the panic stricken disciples reveal about the nature of Christ?

6. In Matthew 17:9, what other majestic event does Jesus say will take place?

Connect

1. Some Jewish rabbis have pointed out that the "burning bush" which Moses saw was an object lesson of both the majesty and the mercy of God. His majesty was manifested in the flaming, potent fire and His mercy was revealed in that the bush was not reduced to ashes. How was Moses on the mountain and Peter, James, and John on the mountain of transfiguration also testimonies of the majesty and mercy of God?

2. How might Moses have described God after being on the mountain surrounded by the glory of God for 40 days and nights?

3. Based upon today's three Bible readings and upon the rest of Scripture, mark the following as "P" proper or "I" improper.
a. ___ Pagaentry in a worship service that draws more attention to the ceremony than to God and His Word and Sacraments
b. ___ Despising solemnity and seriousness toward God in a worship service
c. ___ Despising joyful response to hearing the Gospel of forgiveness and eternal life in a worship service
d. ___ Wearing to a worship service the best that you have
e. ___ Remembering that God is awesome and overpowering in His glory and thanking Him for His Son, Jesus Christ, who gives us the undeserved privilege of one day standing in His presence

4. If you were standing on Mount Sinai with Moses and if you had been with Peter, James, and John when Jesus was transfigured, how would you have felt and acted? Do you agree or disagree with this state-

ment? "How I would feel and act if I were in the presence of God is similar to how I feel and act in worship as prompted by the Holy Spirit."

Vision

During This Week

1. Read Psalms 90–106. Reflect upon two psalms a day. List the descriptions that tell of God's might and of His mercy.

2. Ask yourself as you approach various situations, "Is this how I would act if I were in the presence of God?" By the prompting of the Holy Spirit, pray for God's guidance in all that you do. Be assured also that when you fail to act as a person who lives in the presence of God, that God provides forgiveness through Christ to all repentant sinners.

Closing Worship

Pray together the collect for Transfiguration taken from *LW,* page 31.

> O God, in the glorious transfiguration of Your only-begotten Son You once confirmed the mysteries of the faith by the testimony of the ancient fathers, and in the voice that came from the bright cloud You wondrously foreshowed our adoption by grace. Therefore mercifully make us coheirs with our King of His glory, and bring us to the fullness of our inheritance in heaven; through Jesus Christ, our Lord, who lives and reigns with You and the Holy Spirit, one God, now and forever. Amen.

Scripture Lessons for Next Sunday

Read in preparation for next Sunday Genesis 2:7–9, 15–17; 3:1–7; Romans 5:12 (13–16), 17–19; and Matthew 4:1–11.